Education Revolution

Education
Revolution

A NEW EDUCATION MODEL

FOR

HUMANITY

WILL STANTON

This edition published in 2015 by Will Stanton

ISBN 978-0-9943170-0-1

Cover design by GusTyk with original artwork by Funerium © (www.funerium.deviantart.com)

This book is dedicated to Amelia & Alexander.

I wish you both happiness.

ACKNOWLEDGEMENTS

I want to thank Ethan for being a close friend during this chapter of my journey. This book wouldn't exist if it weren't for him. He was a key part of the process and gave me so much.

I have to also say a big thanks to Renée, who shone her light to help me navigate through the darkness.

Thank you to Lauren, who helped me greatly during the final stages of editing and gave me much-needed feedback.

To Vivienne Stennulat, who reached out and offered her artistic services out of the kindness of her heart. She co-authored a children's book called *The Little Dragon I-Can't* that has a great message for kids about personal growth.

To Joseph Brown, for caring about my mission and giving me an amazing writing platform online.

To my housemates, Nick and Zen, I have to apologise for not being all that present. You guys were both there for me during dark times and I'm so grateful for that.

To my family, who have given me their love and support. It hasn't been easy for them coming to terms with my path, so I thank them for having faith. Love you all dearly.

To everyone else who reached out to me or donated their time or money to the mission, thank you!

CONTENTS

Foreword

This is a book for anyone who cares about the future of education on this planet. It is a book for those who know that we can do so much better for our children. It is a message to all of humanity, but in particular, to those people out there who have the courage and the ferocity to stand in their integrity and fight for what is right.

To the young people reading this book – be wise, be passionate and be fearless. As future custodians of the earth, I hope that you will continue to work towards the liberation of our species and to uphold the values of our ancient indigenous ancestors. The evolution of humanity is in *your* hands.

I ask only that anyone who reads this book does so with an open heart and an open mind.

Introduction

I have been many things in my life. Musician, actor, poker player, waiter, piano teacher, voice-over artist... the list goes on. If you asked me a year ago what I wanted to do with my life, I would have said 'I want to be a primary school teacher,' because I believed that's what I wanted to be. A year ago I was a pre-service teacher in the middle of my degree but something just didn't feel right. I couldn't pinpoint exactly what it was, but it was there - that niggling sense that the pieces of the puzzle didn't quite fit. At university, I felt that I didn't have much in common with the other pre-service teachers and my results were far from exemplary throughout the academic trials of tertiary studies. I met with one of my faculty representatives midway through 2014, who knew I was lacking motivation in many areas of my course, and she asked me, 'Are you sure you want to be a primary school teacher?' Without giving it any real thought, I said 'Yes', even though somewhere deep within myself, my intuition was second-guessing me.

I kept on with my life, with routine, with order, desperately trying to find the motivation to work on my university papers. It never came. My results started to slip again, as they did the previous year and the year before that. I began to feel like a failure. I knew how badly my parents wanted me to graduate, and it hurt me to know that I was hurting them. I couldn't work out why I was such a lore unto myself. I thought I had all the qualities a primary school teacher should have: patience, compassion, understanding, confidence, passion, energy, and above all, I knew I cared deeply about the wellbeing of children.

So why was there this barrier all the time? I didn't understand it so I gave up trying to. Then one day in August of the same year, my life changed. A seed was planted that would transform my life completely. I was having a drink with a friend of mine and he asked me if I'd heard of ayahuasca. I had no idea what he was talking about. He told me it was a liquid medicine extracted from the root of a plant in South America, and that the people who drink it are taken on a journey through their own subconscious. I didn't know what to make of it at first. He told me that this medicine was said to give people a profound connection with nature and all living things. I was skeptical. We both were. Needless to say, it had me very intrigued.

The following day, I decided to do some research on ayahuasca. I read recount after recount of people who had experienced this so-called medicine. I couldn't believe what I was reading. Almost every one of these recounts was saying much the same thing. Most of these people said that they had confronted their own personal demons through an eight hour visual journey into their subconscious, and come out of the other end free of those personal burdens. Many recalled themselves developing a closer bond with the earth and that they felt a great desire to change their lives and help others. I began to look at the scientific studies that were done on ayahuasca to see if the clinical research supported the anecdotal evidence. There weren't many studies, but the ones I did manage to find supported the hypothesis that ayahuasca was of great medicinal value to humans.

Preliminary studies on ayahuasca and drug addiction showed that ayahuasca had the power to overcome alcoholism, cocaine addiction and heroin addiction. So why was the core active ingredient, dimethyltryptamine (DMT) considered a schedule 1 drug in the US? For a drug to be considered schedule 1 in the US it must have no medicinal value or a high potential for abuse. The clinical studies made it very clear that ayahuasca had almost zero abuse potential. The fact that ayahuasca contained DMT made it illegal in the US and almost everywhere else in the world. Why? The shamans who run the ayahuasca ceremonies call it the 'plant teacher' and have sworn by its healing benefits for many generations. I sensed something didn't add up.

I looked at the research on DMT conducted by Dr. Rick Strassman in his book, 'DMT: The Spirit Molecule'. Dr. Strassman discovered that DMT is produced in the pineal gland, and that it is excreted naturally when we dream and during near-death experiences, as well as during birth and death. The pineal gland is located in the centre of the brain.

Buddhists, Taoists and Hindus refer to this gland as the 'third eye'. Others call it the mind's eye. It is believed by many to be connected to the phenomena of spiritual experiences. The 'third eye' is also one of the seven chakras of eastern meditation.

On discovering this connection between the pineal gland and apparent spiritual experiences, it dawned on me that perhaps the reason ayahuasca was illegal in the west was because certain people high up in the power structure didn't like the revelations people were having. I couldn't be certain of course, and I didn't want to jump to any conclusions without looking deeper into it, but it got me thinking. People who reported taking ayahuasca had started to question the system, had a newfound respect for nature and some had even left their high-paid careers for a life of selflessness and a deep desire to give unto others.[1] This can't have been good for the order and the structure of what we call 'the system'. The system relies on jobs that contribute to the growth of the economy. The system relies on compliance to its needs. Ayahuasca was clearly a detriment to the structure of the system. It makes perfect sense that those who control the system would not want to risk a potential destabilising of their power structure. When did humanity get to the stage where we stopped caring about the needs of humanity and only cared about the needs of 'the system?'

---

[1] I want to make something very clear. To this day I have not taken ayahuasca or DMT. I am not telling you to go out and do them. If you do choose to seek them out, do your research first. They are not to be used for recreational purposes and must be treated with the utmost respect.

It was at this point that I started meditating. I wanted to change myself. I wanted to find that part of me that cared about the human plight again. So each night, I took the time to sit on my bed and meditate. In the days following, I felt more relaxed and less open to worry and frustration. The deeper I meditated, the more at peace I was. I soon started experiencing vibrations on reaching what I can only describe as the point of complete weightlessness. On reaching this point I was suddenly able to experience a very profound sensation of bliss. I didn't know where these vibrations were coming from or whether there was a scientific explanation for them. Could they have been connected with spiritual phenomena? I didn't know, but they made me feel at peace, so I knew they were a good thing. Each time that I meditated, the vibrations became more frequent, and filled me with an even greater sense of euphoria.

I met up with my friend again (the one who told me about ayahuasca) and confided in him about the research I'd done on ayahuasca and DMT, and the benefits I was experiencing through meditation. I told him my view as to why I thought ayahuasca was illegal and we both seemed to agree. He then told me to watch a movie called *Zeitgeist*. The suggestion came with a warning. He said, 'People who have watched this documentary have had to pick themselves up off the floor afterwards.' So what did I do? I went straight home and watched *Zeitgeist*...

For those of you reading this who have no idea what *Zeitgeist* is, there are three *Zeitgeist* films. The first is split into three sections of its own. In order, the topics covered are religion, 9/11, and the banking system. The man behind the trilogy, Peter Joseph, put in countless hours of historical research to evidence his claims. I'm not saying that everything is true or to be taken as gospel. I recommend verifying the claims with your own research as I did and coming to your own conclusions. That is very important as you will understand when you read this book.

I can tell you that *Zeitgeist* knocked me clean out of the park. It was a wake-up call. By the film's close, I was in tears. I had never experienced such an outpouring of my own emotions. They were not tears of sadness or anger - they were tears of hope. As the tears continued to gush from my eyes, I began to experience the same vibrations that I'd felt during meditation. Then something truly amazing happened... something I will remember for the rest of my life - the epiphany that those who say they have been enlightened are known to experience. At that moment I knew my purpose... to change the education system in a big way...

My goodness, don't you remember when you went first to school?

... and you went to kindergarten... and in kindergarten the idea was to push along so that you could get into first grade... and then push along so that you could get into second grade and third grade and so on, going up and up...

... and then you went into high school and this was a great transition in life... and now the pressure is being put on; you must get ahead, you must go up the grades and finally be good enough to get to college... and then when you get to college you're still going step by step, step by step... up to the great moment until you're ready to go out into the world...

... and then when you get out into this famous world comes the struggle for success in profession or business... and again there seems to be a ladder before you; something for which you are reaching all the time... and then... suddenly... when you're about forty or forty-five years old in the middle of life, you wake up one day and say 'Huh? I've arrived... and by Joe I feel pretty much the same as I've always felt... in fact I'm not so sure that I don't feel a little bit cheated...'

Alan Watts

The Treadmill

Human beings are curious creatures. We're always running on a treadmill with a fishing line dangling in front of us. On the end of the fishing line, in front of our eyes, but just out of reach, is the word *success*, in neon lights. We're attracted to it, like a moth to a flame, and so we run... we run and we run, but still we just can't get to it.

The desire for success is not something we're born with. It is something we're taught. It begins in early childhood when we strive to get a good report card in our first grade of school. We're told that if we don't progress to the next level we'll be a failure. So we push ourselves hard towards success. We force ourselves to be better because we're motivated by fear. We fear what our parents will say or do to us if we let them down. We fear what our teachers will think of us if we don't perform. We fear what our classmates will think of us if we don't progress like everyone else... but worst of all, we fear what we might think of ourselves if we fail. That fear never goes away all through school. Instead it gets worse. The homework starts piling up... then the tests... then the exams... until we reach our final year of high school; the moment we'd been training for our whole lives up until this point. We're told that our results in this final year of schooling will either make or break our adult lives. Somehow, we get through. We get an offer to go to university or college and the pressure begins mounting again. 'If I don't make it through now, I'll never get a full-time job', we tell ourselves. So we surround ourselves with textbooks and academic literature, drinking coffee to stay awake, desperately reaching for the light at the end of the tunnel.

We graduate and show off our fancy black gowns to our parents. We made it! Now it's time to get employed - get that career we always wanted. We start off at the bottom of the chain of command with a salary to match. 'I better buy a nicer car so I fit in at work,' we tell ourselves. So we buy the car, and in the blink of an eye, much of our hard-earned money is gone. Then there's all of a sudden this pressure to settle down in a house and raise a family. So we strive for that promotion. We settle down with someone in a house with a mortgage and have children. Then we're so focused on work that we lose sight of what really matters, but we have to work in order to provide for the family. So we work hard and exhaust ourselves. By the time our kids want to play with us, we're too tired.

Then our kids grow up and they leave school too. They graduate from college and begin their own career... and we reach retirement age and call it quits. We tell our kids we're ready to spend time with them, but they've moved on with their lives. So we focus our attention on our own life. We book that holiday to Paris or we take a caravan up the east coast. We want to hike up into the mountains but the arthritis is really taking its toll... so we never get there. Our health begins to deteriorate quite rapidly. We take a fall and get a hip replacement. We can't do anything we used to be able to do anymore, and soon our kids put us in a nursing home... where we live out our last moments of life.

This is an example of a successful life to most people. Is this the life we really want? The life we want for our children and our grandchildren?

When John Lennon was five years old, his teacher asked him to write down what he wanted to be when he grew up. 'Happy', he wrote. His teacher told him that he didn't understand the assignment. John said that the teacher didn't understand life.

Doesn't this just sum up everything that is wrong with our education system today? The fact that our lives are defined by this thing called 'career'. We need to wake up and see that schools do not have our best interests at heart; our fundamental rights as living, breathing, creative, loving human beings. Schools are not places of education... they are places of indoctrination, limitation and manipulation.

Education is modelled on the interests of industrialisation.
- Ken Robinson

Ken Robinson's TED (Technology, Entertainment, Design) talk on education entitled 'Changing Education Paradigms' is the most viewed TED talk in the forum's history. In this very compelling speech, Ken compares schools to factories, with 'ringing bells', 'separate facilities' and 'separate subjects'. He says that children are educated through the system in 'batches', organised by age group, or as he jokingly puts it, by their 'date of manufacture'. Except this is not a joke. This is really what is happening, and we've been conditioned to think this is just how life works. Well I've got a news flash for you, this is NOT how life works... not at all... and it's time we learned to see through the veneer of the programming we are receiving via this very same education system!

It's time to take a step back. We need to step outside the box for a minute and actually look at what's going on in this insane system we submit ourselves and our children to. We cannot observe the system from within the mentality of the system. We must change our perspective entirely and evaluate the system from the outside. When we learn to step outside the confines of our programmed reality, we see things for what they truly are...

Allow me to paint a picture of what happens to a child who is churned through the system. The child comes into the world, full of imagination, creative spark and natural verve! What a beautiful gift this life is to the world; full of potential and raw energy. They create, build, draw, sing, run, jump, laugh, invent and inquire. Wow! Now that is something to behold. Then, at about the age of 4 or 5 they go to school. They start to draw but their teacher scolds them for not following instructions. They start to sing but their teacher scolds them for misbehaving. They start to invent but the teacher says, 'You can do that in your own time!' They start to inquire but the teacher says, 'Stop asking questions!' All of a sudden, they are boxed in, and they start to inhibit themselves because they are being punished for their own intuitive instincts. They line up, single file, or in two rows, just like soldiers would in a military drill. Teachers talk *at them*, not *with them*. They are not being listened to or understood. Instead, it is they who have to do all the listening and understanding.

They're given gruelling chores to do at home instead of spending time with their family. We call these chores 'homework'. Like there isn't enough work in school? The imagination is quashed in favour of conformity to rules, order and academic elitism. Children are shovelled information by the truckload and commanded to regurgitate it in the form of tests and exams. The arts are considered an 'extra-curricular' program in most western societies and are treated as inferior to the pursuit of conventional academia. In many third world countries, the arts don't even exist in schools.

The children that do not want to conform to the constraints of modern education are seen as trouble-makers. They are the children who are kept down a year so that they have to suffer an extra year of the stuff. They are the children who are taken to the principal and told sternly to shape up or ship out. Then when they're discarded or 'expelled', they are doubly reprimanded by their own parents and made out to be a failure in life. It's no wonder these children have such difficulties in later life when they experience being told they are a failure by both their school system and their own family. Yet we chalk their noninvolvement down to behavioural problems and we medicate those children. As Ken Robinson says, 'we anaesthetise them'... to fit in with the rest of the mob. These children are not sick. They are perfectly healthy people. It is the system that is sick and these children refuse to be part of a sick system. I don't blame them!

For the children who do meet the approval standards of the education system up until their final year of school, they are faced with the most pressure they have ever felt in their entire lives - final exams. As if being forced to conform isn't enough, teenagers have to go through a terrifying gauntlet of academic trials, and are told that their performance during these trials will determine their success in life. Let me tell you what happened to me in my final year of high school.

At the start of the year my parents got divorced. I had to push that aside and tunnel through my final year of school without allowing myself to become emotionally affected until after my exams were over. It wasn't easy, but I did the work and achieved a final score of 86.1 out of 99.95. To give you an idea of where this score stood, it was around 1 standard deviation above the mean score for the state. To me, and to my parents, it was a good score. I got into a general Arts degree at the prestigious Melbourne University, which turned out to be the biggest waste of time in my life, as I dropped out two years later due to having no interest in pursuing careers that came from a general Arts degree. I changed course to another university to pursue primary education, which required a significantly smaller score as a prerequisite than my 86.1...

and that wasn't to be either. Instead, I decided to drop everything to write this book and to devote my life to changing the educational paradigm.

After all that, did the score matter? Not in the slightest. Do I resent being put under that pressure during a very difficult time in my family life? You bet I do! No child deserves to go through that level of stress - it's inhumane. To all the parents out there whose children are approaching this juncture, tell your kids it's not the end of the world if they don't get a good score. For the most part, they will find a way to do what their heart tells them, regardless of a few numbers on a certificate.

So, what happened during this process we call 'education'? A child was turned from a carefree, imaginative and deeply intuitive human being, to an obedient, conforming, anaesthetised commodity, ready to be shipped off to the next elitist institution, in preparation for a life of further slavery and ownership. The students that didn't make the grade because they either questioned the system or resisted their programming were simply thrown into the discard pile, as they didn't serve the system's needs.

The most obvious indicator that schools are just factories is the growth of standardised testing. This is happening worldwide and only serves to suit 'the State' and the corporations. It has had a damaging effect on schools, teachers and students, and is only getting worse. Standardised testing has a lot of parents and educators worked up, and rightfully it should. It's poisonous to education.

In Australia, the mark of a good school according to the
Australian Curriculum Assessment and Reporting
Authority's (ACARA) MySchool website, *myschool.edu.au*,
is how well that school performed overall on the
government's standardised testing programs. ACARA is
an institutional body controlled by the Australian
Government. It is not an independent educational
organisation. When the government says 'jump', ACARA
says 'how high?'

The fact that schools are directly competing with each
other on the MySchool website for enrolment numbers,
ensures that schools place a great deal of focus on
standardised testing. This leads teachers to do what is
called 'teaching to the test'. This is when they abandon the
standard curriculum for a number of weeks to drill the
students with useless literacy and numeracy problems that
have no bearing on those children's lives, just so they can
get a good result on the standardised tests. The reason the
teachers do this is because their job security is threatened
by poor results in standardised tests.

When I was a pre-service primary school teacher, I
learned that in Australia, teachers in government-run
schools are on one-year contracts. After one year, they
must reapply for their job and face a fair chance of being
replaced and having to find new work. This is a fear they
must face every year. The greatest factor in being rehired
by the school is the teacher's overall results on their class's
standardised tests. This has reached the point of
ridiculousness. Children are being force-fed this stuff and
as soon as the testing is over, they forget it all, because it

wasn't meaningful information in the first place. There have even been times when teachers have been caught cheating, by erasing many of their class's incorrect responses and pencilling in the correct ones. With this much pressure to perform well in these tests, can you really blame them?

I went through these standardised tests all through school, as I'm sure a lot of you reading this book did too, and I can say with conviction that they are absolutely mind-numbing and served no real educational purpose at all. The children of today have it far worse in this regard. Less and less time is devoted to the curriculum, and more and more time is spent preparing these children for the tests. I occasionally teach piano to kids and one of the parents mentioned that her child performed really highly on his NAPLAN test (National Assessment Program – Literacy and Numeracy), and she told him how proud she was. I held my tongue of course, but for me it was a sobering moment - the moment reality sunk in. With just one simple remark from a parent I could see how bad things had become. I don't think ill of her at all for saying that. It has become a normal part of the societal zeitgeist, and I don't blame the parents for their lack of protest. I blame the system that frowns upon anyone who challenges the current paradigm. That is at the heart of the issue. Anyone who steps outside of convention is seen as a threat to the system. All that said, standardised testing has no place in the realm of education. Since when is a child's intelligence or educational merit dictated by a silly multiple choice quiz? Schools are there to educate, not stupefy.

This factory model has to end for the sake of the wellbeing of future generations and the evolution of humanity itself. We need to stop running endlessly on the treadmill and realise it's a road to nowhere. Only when we step off the treadmill do we truly begin to understand what life is all about. As you will see throughout the various chapters of this book, our progress is being held back by the system and we're turning our kids into machines when we need to be unleashing their true potential as human beings.

It's time to wake up...

It is well that the people of the nation do not understand our banking and monetary system, for if they did, I believe there would be a revolution before tomorrow morning.

Henry Ford

Sleight of Hand

Many of us take pause in our lives to question the nature of our existence. It is an important curiosity to nurture, after all, if we want to derive meaning from life. Who are we? Where did we come from? How did our universe come into being?

But have you ever taken pause to ask where money came from? Who prints it? How did it come into being? Seeing as money dictates what kind of job we have, our living arrangements, and our very survival in modern society, people ought to know the truth about those decorative pieces of paper in our purses and wallets.

In the United States, and indeed almost everywhere around the world, the money supply is controlled by central banks. The most prominent of these central banks to be introduced into the US was the Federal Reserve Bank, which came into existence in 1913 at the time Woodrow Wilson was President.

The Federal Reserve is not owned or controlled by the government. It is a privately owned bank that controls both

inflation (the money supply) and **interest**. There is
absolutely nothing federal about the Federal Reserve Bank.

*Some people think that the Federal Reserve Banks are United
States Government institutions. They are private monopolies
which prey upon the people of these United States for the benefit
of themselves and their foreign customers; foreign and domestic
speculators and swindlers; and rich and predatory money
lenders.*

- Louis T. McFadden, Chairman of the House Banking and
Currency Committee, from a speech on June 10, 1932 to Floor of
House of Representatives

In his book, *With No Apologies* (1979), Senator Barry
Goldwater writes:

*Most Americans have no real understanding of the operation of
the international money lenders. The accounts of the Federal
Reserve System have never been audited. It operates outside the
control of Congress and manipulates the credit of the United
States.*

So, if the Federal Reserve Bank is a private institution that
controls the money supply, how does the money supply
come into existence? The answer - the Fed creates money
out of thin air. It then loans that newly created money to
the government **at interest**. That money is then filtered
through the economy, which eventually makes its way to
the people. When the government needs more money, they
borrow even more money from the Fed, **at interest**, which

the Fed of course creates out of nothing as well. If you haven't already figured it out, this only produces one thing - perpetual **debt**. Where does the government get the money to pay the interest on those loans? Nowhere, because there isn't enough money in circulation to pay back that interest. It doesn't exist. So the inevitable debt cycle begins. The more money the government loans from the Fed, the more debt it accrues. The more debt the government accrues, the more money it has to loan from the Fed. This debt-based monetary system was outlined in a document released in the last decade by the Federal Reserve Bank entitled *Modern Money Mechanics*.

The document states:

They [the banks] do not really pay out loans from the money they receive as deposits. If they did this, no additional money would be created. What they do when they make loans is to accept promissory notes in exchange for credits to the borrowers' transaction accounts.

Put simply, the Fed (and all other central banks) accepts IOUs (promissory notes) from the government in exchange for money (credits). Thus, money is created out of debt.

Theodore Thoren and Richard Warner, two men with extensive backgrounds in mechanical engineering and mathematics, outlined this process of money creation by the Federal Reserve, in *The Truth in Money Book* (1980):

Congress votes to increase the federal debt limit, let us say by $1 billion, and instructs the US Treasury to write an interest-bearing bond for $1 billion. The Treasury offers to sell the bond to the Fed. The Fed buys the bond by simply creating a bookkeeping entry for $1 billion to the credit of the government's checking account. The Treasury now writes checks against the created credit. These checks are dispersed throughout the country, endorsed by recipients and deposited into banks.

These 'bonds' are nothing more than worthless pieces of paper the government instructs the treasury to draw up, with some fancy logos and a few pictures, that it gives to the Fed in exchange for a line of credit.

So what about the debt, who pays it? The citizens do. A large percentage of the average American's hard-earned money goes back to the Fed, who can just create more money out of thin air anyway. The end result is total slavery of the nation's citizens to the bankers who run the show.

People have been trying to expose the Federal Reserve pyramid scheme for a long time. Louis McFadden, a long-time opponent of the banking cartels, said in a speech to Congress in 1932:

When the Federal Reserve Act was passed, the people of the United States did not perceive that a world banking system was being set up here. A superstate controlled by international bankers and industrialists acting together to enslave the world for their own pleasure. Every effort has been made to conceal its powers but the truth is - the Fed has usurped the government.

Ron Paul knew the damage the Federal Reserve could do to the global economy and openly spoke out against the Fed during his presidential campaigns in 2012 and 2014. In his book, *End the Fed*, Paul wrote:

When we unplug the Fed, the dollar will stop its long depreciating trend, international currency values will stop fluctuating wildly, banking will no longer be a dice game, and financial power will cease to gravitate toward a small circle of government-connected insiders.

How did such a dangerous bill get past Congress in the first place? To understand this, we have to go back to 1910, when the idea was first conceived by a group of seven men (some Wall Street bankers, others politicians), who met in secret to discuss the creation of such a system, and had intimate ties to the four dominant banking families of the world - the Warburgs, the Morgans, the Rockefellers and the Rothschilds.

Senator Nelson Aldrich, Paul Warburg, Abraham Andrew, Henry Davison, Benjamin Strong, Frank Vanderlip and Charles Norton, met on a piece of land off the coast of Georgia called Jekyll Island. Vanderlip later recorded the train journey south from New Jersey in his autobiography, *From Farm Boy to Financier* (1935):

I do not feel it is any exaggeration to speak of our secret expedition to Jekyll Island as the occasion of the actual conception of what eventually became the Federal Reserve System...

We were told to leave our last names behind us. We were told, further, that we should avoid dining together on the night of our departure. We were instructed to come one at a time and as unobtrusively as possible to the railroad terminal on the New Jersey littoral of the Hudson, where Senator Aldrich's private car would be in readiness, attached to the rear end of a train for the south.

When I came to that car the blinds were down and only slender threads of amber light showed the shape of the windows. Once aboard the private car we began to observe the taboo that had been fixed on last names. We addressed each other as Ben, Paul, Nelson, Abe (it is Abram Piatt Andrew). Davison and I adopted even deeper disguises, abandoning our own first names. On the theory that we were always right, he became Wilbur and I became Orville, after those two aviation pioneers, the Wright brothers. Incidentally, for years afterward Davison and I continued the practice, in communications, and when we were together.

The servants and the train crew may have known the identities of one or two of us, but they did not know all, and it was the names of all printed together that would have made our mysterious journey significant in Washington, in Wall Street, even in London. Discovery, we knew, simply must not happen, or else all our time and effort would be wasted. If it were to be exposed publicly that our particular group had gotten together and written a banking bill, that bill would have no chance whatever of passage by Congress.

Vanderlip went on to write of the time the men spent on Jekyll Island:

We were taken by boat from the mainland to Jekyll Island and for a week or ten days were completely secluded, without any contact by telephone or telegraph with the outside. We had disappeared from the world onto a deserted island. There were plenty of colored servants but they had no idea who Ben and Paul and Nelson were; even Vanderlip, or Davison, or Andrew, would have meant less than nothing to them. There we worked in the club-house – We returned to the north as secretly as we had gone south.

Woodrow Wilson became Governor of New Jersey in 1910 and later ran for President of the United States. During his presidential campaign, Wilson received a majority of his campaign funding from Wall Street bankers who had direct connections to the men who met on Jekyll Island. He became President of the United States in 1912. Wilson's top adviser and mentor, Colonel Edward House, had interests with the banking cartels, and succeeded in manipulating Wilson to bring about the new bill.

Antony C. Sutton, former Research Fellow at Stanford University, wrote in his account of the conception of the Federal Reserve:

In March (1913), Frank Vanderlip talked with House, and two weeks later a group of bankers arrived at the White House with a printed 'currency reform' bill for Wilson to present to Congress.

The bill, titled the Federal Reserve Act, was passed through Congress in 1913. Woodrow Wilson, later realising the ramifications of what he had done, wrote:

...there has come about an extraordinary and very sinister concentration in the control of business in the country... however it has come about, it is more important still that the control of credit also has become dangerously centralized...

The great monopoly in this country is the monopoly of big credits. So long as that exists, our old variety and freedom and individual energy of development are out of the question.

A great industrial nation is controlled by its system of credit. Our system of credit is privately concentrated. The growth of the nation, therefore, and all our activities are in the hands of a few men... who, by very reason of their own limitations, chill and check and destroy genuine economic freedom.

- Woodrow Wilson,

The New Freedom: A Call for the Emancipation of the Generous Energies of a People (1913)

The founding fathers of America forewarned of the potentially disastrous consequences of a central banking monopoly, and were strongly opposed to such systems being put in place.

And I sincerely believe, with you, that banking establishments are more dangerous than standing armies; and that the principle of spending money to be paid by posterity in the name of funding, is but swindling futurity on a large scale.

- Thomas Jefferson, in a letter to John Taylor in 1816

History records that the money changers have used every form of abuse, intrigue, deceit and violent means possible to maintain their control over governments by controlling money and its issuance.

- James Madison, in *The Writings of James Madison* (1783-1787)

Given that the Federal Reserve banking system causes a never-ending debt spiral, it would be safe to say that the US National Debt is fairly high. How high? At the time of writing this book, the debt clock stands at approximately:

$17,700,000,000,000

For those of you who get a bit lost among the zeros, that's 17.7 trillion US dollars. Not billion, trillion...

What happens when the Federal Reserve calls in the debt? Complete global economic panic. The US economy would be brought to its knees and international economies along with it. It would be the worst financial disaster in the world's history. What's to stop the Fed calling in their loans anytime? Absolutely nothing. Remember, these banking cartels do not operate in the interests of the government or in the interests of the people. They operate purely out of the interest of their own monopoly as they are the men at the very top of the pyramid. They have the power to cripple nations by controlling the issuance of currency.

It is important to note that since the conception of the Federal Reserve Bank, the world has adopted similar private central banking systems that follow the same credit-controlling model, independent of governments. Even before the Federal Reserve, the UK had a central bank of its own, the Bank of England. The Bank of England's 2008 quarterly bulletin states:

Banks extend credit by creating money.

Again... by creating money out of **nothing**. Almost every country in the world has a central bank that controls the credit of that country in this way. In Australia, there is the Reserve Bank of Australia. In New Zealand, the Reserve Bank of New Zealand. In Canada, the Bank of Canada. In Germany, Deutsche Bundesbank. In Malaysia, the Central Bank of Malaysia. It is in your interests to find out which central bank prints **your** country's money and controls **your** country's government.

Reginald McKenna, Chairman of the Board of the Midland Bank, reportedly told his stockholders in 1924:

I am afraid the ordinary citizen will not like to be told that the banks can, and do, create money... And they who control the credit of the nation direct the policy of Governments and hold in the hollow of their hands the destiny of the people.

The Federal Reserve Bank has been exposed for quite some time but the average global citizen has no idea of the scam it is running, due to the lack of media attention surrounding the Fed, and they deserve to know what's really going on!

There is currently a global 'End the Fed' movement happening. It started with Ron Paul's political campaign for President in 2012 and has snowballed from there. In Germany, the movement has taken on huge proportions. In June of 2014, the website *wearechange.org* released a video showing thousands of demonstrators of all ages and from all walks of life engaging in peaceful protest in the heart of Berlin, to raise awareness of the Federal Reserve Bank and the negative impact it is having on the world economy. The main organiser of the protests, Lars Maehrholz, says that the problem is not just the Fed, but the way banks operate on an international level.

The other public face of the movement in Germany is Ken Jebsen, who was a mainstream news reporter for more than 20 years. He says that he was fired for asking too many questions on hard-hitting issues in his reports. Ken and Lars both say that after the movement started gaining real momentum, the mainstream German news outlets took to smearing their reputations and went as far as to label them 'Nazis'. In the video, they both state that they abhor war and are striving for peace in the world.

In many countries around the world, including the United States, the United Kingdom and Australia, money used to be backed by gold or was redeemable in gold. The gold standard has since been abolished globally. This means that our money is absolutely worthless. It is backed by nothing. It has no value. It is **fiat** money. Central banks just slap the words 'legal tender' on it and all of a sudden it has the **illusion** of value. Money is quite literally worthless paper, but the world has been conned into thinking otherwise.

The way our monetary system is set up allows banking institutions to control the status quo, instead of giving the power to the people where it rightfully belongs. So long as money remains in existence, there will always be bankers who take advantage. Money is at the root of all the suffering in the world and there is a hell of a lot of suffering in this world! Money is the reason so many people die of starvation every day. Money is the reason the 'middle classes' are being made obsolete to make the rich even richer and the poor even poorer. Money is the reason the needs of the planet are being completely ignored, because profit margins are more important to our 'masters' than basic human values and the state of the natural world.

The reason I have devoted an entire chapter to this is because I am certain the world would be a better place without money altogether. It enslaves us. It enslaves our children, and if we don't strive for a world free of money, it will enslave the human race indefinitely. I for one cannot sit back and allow humanity to suffer through to its extinction. It is paramount that the world takes steps to move in the direction of a new system that does not use money, and therefore the education system must reflect this.

If you want to continue to be the slaves of bankers and pay the cost of your own slavery, then let bankers continue to create money and control credit.

- Sir Josiah Stamp, Bank of England President, in an informal speech to professors at the University of Texas, 1927

Money is an illusion. It has no power. We, the people, have the real power! The African tribes-people live their lives by a simple philosophy. It's called Ubuntu, which translates to 'I am because we are'. We don't need money to progress as a human race. Money controls us. We don't need it to live a happy life. We just need to work together and make sure that no one is allowed to suffer. We can create a world that works on this Ubuntu philosophy, but much more on that later in the book.

In order to free ourselves, we must first recognise that right now we are slaves to this system. Only then can we break the chains that bind us and create the world we want to see...

In almost every act of our daily lives, whether in the sphere of politics or business, in our social conduct or our ethical thinking, we are dominated by a relatively small number of persons – who understand the mental processes and social patterns of the masses. It is they who pull the wires that control the public mind.

Edward Bernays

Education is what remains after one has forgotten what one has learned in school.

Albert Einstein

The essence of the independent mind lies not in what it thinks, but in how it thinks.

Christopher Hitchens

Thought Control

I f you are disillusioned by the state of our current global education system, and you're not alone by any stretch I assure you, chances are this is one of the issues that really hits home for you. This issue is perhaps the single-most important issue facing education today. I am talking about **the absence of critical thinking.**

The very fact that it has taken me seven years after leaving school to really question the system we are in is testament to this. Schools expect children to swallow information and never question anything they are being fed. In no way is that considered learning. That is called indoctrination, plain and simple, and if we want our children to hold dominion over their own minds, this cannot be allowed to continue.

Teachers are hardly teaching at all. They are merely repeating what they were 'taught' when they were first indoctrinated; they are perpetuating a cycle of programming that is not nurturing the cognitive, emotional and spiritual needs of our children, and instead is limiting their potential immensely. It's not the teachers' fault. They don't know any better, and for the most part, their hearts are in the right place. I was on track to be one of them. I thought I was doing it for all the right reasons, and in hindsight, I guess I *was* doing it for all the right reasons... but I never questioned what it was I was actually doing. What are we actually teaching these brave kids who are ready and willing to learn about this beautiful, majestic thing we call 'life'?

When it really comes down to it, we're teaching our children to obey - to accept authority as truth, instead of truth as authority.

I remember when I was a student in high school and one of my mathematics teachers was explaining a brand new concept to the class. When the teacher finished explaining what the concept was, and made sure it was clearly understood, one of my classmates raised his hand. The teacher prompted him to speak, and he said, 'I understand how it all works, but *why* does it work?' The teacher didn't have an explanation. Instead, the response was, 'I don't know, it just does.' This is not a dig at my high school mathematics teacher. As I said before, this is not a fault of the teachers, but a much larger problem that concerns the most fundamental machinations of the system itself. The teachers are just symptoms of a great sickness in our current educational paradigm.

Teachers have been pre-programmed, through their own experiences as pupils, to assert their authority over knowledge, without questioning the knowledge at all. So it becomes a cyclical process. The children consume what they are being fed and then some of those children become teachers who then tell the next lot of children to consume what they are being fed. The children who question what they are being fed are not having their questions answered, but instead being told not to be so inquisitive and to get on with the task at hand. So these children learn to stop asking questions. This has destructive consequences for the future of these children, and those consequences are far-reaching, and can be seen in the very way society is operating today, above and beyond the traditional educational arena.

What we see happening in schools is happening in exactly the same way in other institutions, they just 'appear' unrelated. What is the mainstream media, if not just another 'education' platform asserting authority as truth? We sit down in front of the nightly news and listen to anchors and reporters tell us what to think, who to point our finger at, why our country needs to go to war, and what we should be terrified of. Very few of us question them. Why is that? Because they wear well-pressed suits, pretty dresses, are extremely well organised, are supported by whiz-bang graphics and a dramatic musical score, and speak with a stylised voice they learned at broadcasting school? The reality is that these mainstream news sources are owned by giant corporations. These corporations have one bottom line - profit. Any journalism that doesn't align with their profit-agenda is not worthy of being news, so it doesn't make the cut. What we end up seeing is a completely skewed version of events, and in some cases, a completely false version of events.

Wars are only initiated or joined by a country once the
public consensus agrees on going to war. If an
overwhelming majority of people in a country were
strongly against going to war, and the leaders went to war
anyway, those leaders would be chased down the street!
How do you get a country to support a war? Politicians
can't do it alone because people are becoming wise to the
game of politics. They need the media on their side.

Just to show you how controlled the media is in the
USA alone, consider the following. In 1983, 90% of
American media was owned by 50 companies. Today, that
same 90% is controlled by **6 companies**. The six companies
are News-Corp, Comcast, Viacom, Disney, CBS and Time
Warner.

Below is a list of just some of the American media these
six companies control.

News-Corp:	Fox, Wall Street Journal, New York Post
Comcast:	NBC, Universal Pictures, Focus Features
Viacom:	MTV, Nick Jr., BET, CMT, Paramount Pictures
Disney:	ABC, ESPN, Pixar, Miramax, Marvel Studios
CBS:	Showtime, Smithsonian Channel, NFL.com, 60 Minutes
Time Warner:	CNN, HBO, Time, Warner Bros

As an Australian (and this is for the benefit of the
Australian readers), I want to add that News-Corp also
controls:

*The Australian, Herald Sun, mX (Melbourne), The Daily
Telegraph, The Advertiser, The Courier-Mail,
www.news.com.au,* and the *Australian Associated Press.*

In the UK, News-Corp owns:

The Sun, The Times, and the *Press Association.*

Keep in mind when you're reading any of these news sources that the person who decides what goes in them, Rupert Murdoch, is the same person responsible for the Fox News Network. You know, Fox News, the same network that gave Bill O'Reilly and Sean Hannity a platform for peddling bigotry and xenophobia.

It doesn't matter what news network you watch or what newspaper you read, it is so important to question it all! I can't stress that enough. Don't blindly accept it as the truth just because they tell you to. You need to conduct your own inquiries on the matter. Read what the independent news sources have to say on the same issue. Do the research yourself and weigh the evidence. Ask things like, 'Who controls this media source? Is there a profit-agenda behind it? Do the owners have any ties to government or politicians? Is this an objective report? Are they showing us the full story? What *aren't* they reporting? Are they attempting to empower or disempower?'

That goes for anything I say in this book, too. Hold me to account. I am not an authority on truth. I urge you to verify any claims I have made, particularly on the Federal Reserve Bank in the previous chapter, and discover the facts for yourself. Examine all the evidence and reach your own informed conclusion. That is at the heart of all of this. The reason we are so blindly allowing our media and our politicians to dictate how we should feel about matters of public interest is because we have been educated from a very early age to accept the voice of authority as the voice of reason.

Another institution that seeks to assert its authority over us is the advertising industry. Children are being bombarded by advertising from all directions from the moment they learn to decode basic language. Their sense of personal and social adequacy is relentlessly attacked by corporations that wish to profit by exploiting these children. Children aren't born insecure. Advertising makes them that way by scaring the hell out of them. They tell young boys that they won't be 'cool' if they don't own the latest gadgetry, and young girls that they won't be 'pretty' if they don't start wearing make-up. Advertising sets up the greatest prison of all - the fear of what other people think. We care so much about what others think of us that we censor ourselves and quash our own expressions to the point of unhappiness. Advertising tells us we are not good enough the way we are, and this is simply not true. We are amazing people capable of the most extraordinary things... each and every one of us!

I have had first-hand experience within the advertising industry. I was in it for nearly two years. I have been on the other side of the television screen and the radio as a voice-over artist. It's a cut-throat world all about understanding how the consumer thinks. As someone who helped create the ads, I had to put myself in the shoes of the consumer in order to understand their desires, wants and needs. It dehumanises people. The advertising industry doesn't see people as living, breathing, loving human beings. It sees them as cattle, branded by which target market they belong to. The words 'target market' should be a giveaway as to why advertising is such an inhumane industry, as it implies that human beings are merely prey being hunted by these corporations - and that's exactly what is happening. I have now decided I do not wish to participate in the industry any longer.

When I was training as a pre-service teacher in a Melbourne primary school, my supervising teacher had come up with an activity for the Grade 2 class that required the children to design their own ad for a toy. The objective was to persuade the other children in the class to want to buy their toy, so to prepare them my supervising teacher played a handful of commercial TV ads to the class. This was an ongoing project to be completed over several days. The following day, my supervising teacher called in sick, and the school organised a young male replacement teacher to come. I was not allowed to have full control of the class at this stage in my training. When it came time for the children to work on their toy ads, the replacement teacher told the children to sit in a circle in front of him. He then began to explain to the children that advertising was telling them what to buy and what to think, and the importance of questioning the messages ads were sending them. At the time, I remember thinking to myself, 'These kids don't want to know this!'

Looking back, I realise how programmed I was. The replacement teacher had it right. Why is this kind of necessary dialogue considered taboo in schools? If we're not going to talk about it in schools, where are we going to talk about it? These discussions don't seem to be happening at home, as kids are still passively learning to be good little consumers and never appear to grow out of the habit. If we're really going to educate our children, we have to teach them the importance of thinking for themselves, and that includes teaching them to question media and advertising.

To better understand how critical thinking is discouraged in the standardised education system, we need to look at the way history is taught in schools. Most of us never really think twice about the validity of what we were taught in history class, but this is where one of the greatest indoctrinations of our children is taking place, and it has disastrous consequences for our future. It is time we confronted this reality.

> *Those who tell the stories rule society.*
> - Plato

> *The very concept of objective truth is fading out of the world. Lies will pass into history.*
> - George Orwell

According to our teachers and textbooks, the history that our children are taught in schools is our true history. It is stated as fact, and never opens itself up for investigation or scrutiny within the academic arena. How do we know that what we're taught in history is what really happened? How do we know that conventional history does not omit important details that may be crucial in piecing the puzzle together? The simple answer to these questions is *we don't.* So if we don't know that our history could be doctored in many ways, why do we teach it as fact? History, by its very nature, can only ever really be speculation. History should not be taught by ramming a single narrative down the children's throats. After all, whose narrative is it, the government's? Or is it the narrative that was reported in the mainstream press? Regardless of where it came from, it doesn't make it true. It doesn't necessarily make it false either. The fact that we don't know for sure means that we simply cannot teach history in this way.

Should history be taught at all in schools? Let's not forget this quote, often misattributed to Churchill:

Those who cannot remember the past are condemned to repeat it.
- George Santayana

History definitely has a place in schools, as we must learn from the past, but we have to rework the way in which it is taught. We must accept that there are alternate explanations for particular events that occurred, and are occurring in this world. We must accept that a large percentage of people reject the official narrative of the World Trade Centre disasters of 9/11, including thousands of architects and engineers who are still demanding a more thorough investigation. We must also accept that there are still many people who don't believe Lee Harvey Oswald, the supposed lone-lunatic gunman, assassinated John F Kennedy.

It is not for me to say which side of the fence I am on, or to try to bring you over to my side, on any of these world events. That doesn't matter. What matters is that we open up a dialogue in history classes that does not out-right reject alternate explanations. Many of these alternate explanations are well-evidenced and well-researched. Therefore, it is paramount that we weigh this evidence also, as there are always two sides to every story. History must be taught by looking at both sides of the coin, by looking at *all* the evidence, and most importantly, by providing our children with the *tools* to conduct their own investigations and reach their own conclusions. Only then will we be truly fostering their capacity for critical thought in this subject.

Now, as this chapter is so heavily focused on the indoctrination going on in our schools, I feel I must mention the elephant in the room - religion. I am going to be quite brief as I have a very clear stand-point on this with regard to the school environment. I don't care if parents teach religion to their children at home. They have every right to do so. However.... **religion does not have any place in schools**. I am not a militant atheist, nor do I really consider myself an atheist at all. Schools are not in the business of telling people what to believe. They are about educating children. The term 'religious education' or RE is a complete and total fallacy. Teaching a child religion within the school environment is not educating that child, it is *brainwashing* that child. If a child wants to follow a religion, they should do so of their own volition, and not because the education system tells them to.

If we are to prevent the indoctrination of future generations, we need to rethink our entire approach to teaching; we need to change the game altogether. There are those who argue that critical thinking cannot be taught in schools. To them I say, 'Think outside the box!' You cannot teach children to think critically by saying, 'This is how you think critically.' If you approach it in this way it will not work. The great Athenian philosopher, Socrates, knew this.

I cannot teach anybody anything - I can only make them think.
                              - Socrates

Socrates also knew that the way to educate people was by asking questions and not by giving answers. The solution is to adopt a philosophical approach. John L. Taylor explains this approach in his book, *Think Again: A Philosophical Approach to Teaching.*

Teaching philosophically should happen by a process I call 'Socratic mentoring', in which, like Socrates, we probe and challenge our students, questioning the things they say, and stimulating the intellectually somnolent to begin thinking for themselves.

It's not just the act of asking questions that matters, but the type of questions we ask. The best questions are not those that can be answered immediately. The best questions are the ones that give pause; that make students take that all-important step back and look inwardly. The *self* is the real teacher, not the person asking the questions. It is up to us to challenge our students to look within themselves for the answer, but just as importantly, we need to allow our students to challenge us. It's about time we break down the barriers between the teachers and the students, and be willing to accept that we are not the authority on truth. I am not saying that teachers need to denounce all authority. That would make behaviour management very difficult. I am saying that we need to stop talking at the kids, and start talking *with* them. The age of the information dictator is over. The time for open dialogue is here.

Let's not stop there. Let's also acknowledge the importance of teaching *philosophy* itself in schools. Being able to take a step back from it all and to look at things through a different lens is an immensely valuable skill for humans to have. Look at the world right now. Look at the big picture for a moment. There are millions of innocent men, women and children having their lives torn apart by the Military Industrial Complex in every way imaginable. Millions more are dying because they don't have the basic human needs for survival - they don't have access to food, shelter and clean drinking water. The richest 1% of the global population accounts for 46% of the world's wealth, and the gap is only widening. We have the power to fix all of these problems, yet the vast majority of us turn a blind eye because it doesn't appear to impact on our small spheres of existence. We're programmed by the system to have this 'tunnel vision' in life, where the only things that matter are ourselves, our family, our close friends, our money, our material possessions, our security, and paying our taxes on time.

It's great that people care so much about their family and friends. It shows that we really do care about others, but we have to stop thinking that we're all separate from each other, and start realising that we're all in this together. We were all born on the same planet. Each and every one of us has a story. We are not defined by our postcode, or by our class, or by our individuality. We are defined by our *unity*, and somewhere down the line, humanity has forgotten this. Once in a while we have to be able to observe humanity's actions, to look at our place in this universe amongst all intelligence, and to see that there is so much more to this thing we call 'existence' than we ordinarily care to acknowledge. A study of philosophy helps greatly in achieving this.

Philosophy equips our minds with the tools to question our own rigid belief systems. Belief systems are poisonous, no matter what it is that people believe, because the presence of such a system shows complete disregard for its inverse. The only way for us to evolve out of this competitive mess of separation and division that we're in is to accept that our beliefs may be mistaken, and to stop trying to win all our battles. If we direct more attention to philosophy within the education system our children will grow up with the skills needed to open themselves up to the opinions of others and admit to uncertainty.

One of the best lessons to take away from a basic introduction to philosophy is the realization that, however certain your convictions, subjective certainty does not imply truth. You may be mistaken. The probability of disagreement turning into conflict is lowered if dogmatic certainty is tempered by this recognition.

- John L. Taylor

Without critical thinking in this world we would not have people who go against the grain. In times of suffering such as now we need those people more than anything. This skill can be learned and it will be learned, but it won't happen if we remain on our current trajectory. A dramatic shift in the functioning of education must occur if we are to ensure that future generations have full control over their minds. We must face the reality that the State is stealing our kids and engineering them into conforming tools for economic productivity. They are indoctrinated to believe that the mainstream media has their best interests at heart, that material wealth has real value, that their deity is the only true deity, and that authority is legitimacy. I won't stand for the indoctrination any longer. It is time to abolish religious dogmas in schools. It is time to start working with our children instead of against them. It is time to implement a philosophical approach to teaching. It is time to teach more than one version of history. It is time to teach children *how* to think, not what to think.

It is time to take back our minds...

Our current education system systematically drains the creativity out of our children.

Ken Robinson

Educating the mind without educating the heart is no education at all.

Aristotle

Educating the Heart

One of the great tragedies of the current conformist model of education is that vast numbers of children are being ripped away from the things that are most intuitive to them as human beings. They are then forced to undergo a traditional academic approach to learning and are judged on their value in this way. Those who perform poorly under this approach are deemed failures, and then find themselves caught in a downward spiral of self-doubt, self-loathing and self-rejection that is extremely difficult to emerge from.

Everybody is a genius, but if you judge a fish by its ability to climb a tree, it will live its whole life believing it is stupid.

- Anon

The reality is that these children are not failures at all. In fact they are quite the contrary. It is the system itself that fails. These children are simply never given the chance to flourish because the education system stubbornly keeps trying to push square pegs into round holes.

Why must we keep insisting that education is primarily academic in nature? Why is there a hierarchical structure of education that places academia at the top and the arts at the bottom? Learning takes many forms. Children do not all learn in the same way. You cannot seat them all behind desks in a classroom, dictate information to them and expect them to absorb all of it like a sponge. Some will do well learning in this way. A great deal will not. The latter of these children prefer to learn with their bodies, with their hearts and with their imaginations. They are the artists, the dancers, the gymnasts, the runners, the singers, the actors, the writers, the sculptors, the musicians and the visionaries. They are absolutely wonderful people who give so much joy and happiness to others, yet we do not value them as we should. Instead, we reprimand them for not fitting in with the other mob.

A year ago I visited Nepal and taught briefly in a government school in the heart of Kathmandu. As a pre-service teacher at the time I was given this opportunity through an optional program called the Global Experience Placement program. The school I was at was very limited in resources. They had no coloured pencils and writing paper was scarce. The school also taught strictly by rote and aside from a physical education class, everything else was based in academia. Throughout my time observing and teaching the '6th Form' class there were two students, a boy and a girl, who 'acted out' more than any of the other students. They were constantly misbehaving, talking when told not to, and being scolded by all the subject teachers. When I got up to teach in front of the class, I wanted to show the kids a little about Australia, my country of origin. I showed them pictures of native Australian fauna, gave out coloured pencils and had them create their own drawings of one of those animals. It was an introductory icebreaker lesson to get to know the class a little better and for them to get to know me a little better. Some of the children surprised me with their artistic ability, but two of the drawings really stood out and blew the other drawings out of the water. It turned out these were done by the same two poorly behaved students I mentioned earlier. This was not the only time I had seen this in my teaching rounds. I experienced the same thing in a government school in Melbourne with another poorly behaved individual who was an exceptional artist.

Is it really any surprise that these children are poorly behaved? They are clearly talented in other areas that the education system generally neglects and ignores. I argue that this 'acting out' is just their way of expressing the need to have their real interests nurtured. This need is not being met. Instead, these children are being squeezed very uncomfortably into a mould that feels artificial and unnatural.

I think most people on earth have an interest in something or a passion for something - something that makes them tick. Even if people don't know what it is that makes them tick, I think that it's deep within them, waiting to be unearthed.

Ken Robinson calls this the 'element'. In his book, *The Element: How Finding Your Passion Changes Everything*, he describes it as 'the place where the things you love to do and the things that you are good at come together.' Ken is a strong advocate for change in the way that children learn in an educational setting. He writes:

Most students never get to explore the full range of their abilities and interests. Those students whose minds work differently – and we're talking about many students here; perhaps even the majority of them – can feel alienated from the whole culture of education...

Education is the system that's supposed to develop our natural abilities and enable us to make our way in the world. Instead, it is stifling the individual talents and abilities of too many students and killing their motivation to learn.

I spent a great deal of my life being a jack-of-all-trades, master-of-none type guy. In this way, I suppose I became quite well-rounded, but it wasn't until I was twenty five when I found my own 'element'. I like to think of it as my purpose in life; as something I was born to do. It came to me in no less than an epiphany, but when it arrived, it seemed like my whole life had been preparing me for this trailblazing path. It was just up to me to recognise what life was preparing me to venture into, and to connect all the dots of my past together. When I realised my true potential for this life, and what it was I was really capable of, I just couldn't allow myself to be a working cog in the machine. I know that I'm capable of changing education for the better, and my heart is telling me to give every fibre of my being to this cause. So I am. It hasn't been easy for my family to come to grips with, and it is a very lonely path to walk, but I know it is something I must do, and I have come to terms with the sacrifices I have had to make to pursue it.

This revelation has taught me an important lesson about following one's own heart. It is better to take big risks in order to be true to yourself than to play it safe and to never know what could have been.

The system doesn't like to operate on this understanding. It just wants to turn children into obedient workers; workers who keep the machine running at full capacity, with only material wealth as reward. It has been said by many, and I agree, that material wealth is illusory wealth. Happiness is the key to real wealth.

> *Contentment is the most excellent wealth.*
> - Buddha

It is my view that in order to be wholly content one must be in their element. The problem with the education system is that it does not allow children the opportunities to discover and work with their element. Of course, there is the opposing argument that if we all dropped everything to pursue our interests then there would be no one to do the jobs that everyone hates. This is a good thing! At the rate technology is increasing, machines will be able to take on the mundane and menial work that does not serve the soul. This is to be embraced, not feared. Machines are precision instruments. They will do these jobs with superior accuracy to humans and will never have a problem with the sameness of it. It is the concept of money that holds us back. Money restricts progress - it limits what humans are capable of in immense ways. I will come back to this in chapters 5 and 9.

So, how can we help school children find what it is they are truly passionate about? One of the ways we can do this is by allowing them the freedom to explore their creative impulses without restriction. For primary (elementary) schoolers, a certain amount of time should be allocated for *creative play*. In a classroom setting, the children would be given free reign over a wide range of resources and tools, and it would be up to them to use those resources in any way they saw fit. This is when children would really get an opportunity to interact with a blank canvas in every way imaginable and to discover the power of their own creativity. It is about letting their imaginations run wild and giving them a real chance to express themselves. This is a time for teachers to engage with the children on a personal level, provide feedback and encouragement, and to find out more about each child's interests. A good teacher will be able to recognise ability and passion, and strive to nurture that in a child as it becomes apparent.

It is not so easy to apply play-based learning to a secondary school environment, but I think similar outcomes would be achieved through inquiry-based learning as discussed in the previous chapter. Creative play would be most effective for primary-age learners and it would be beneficial in helping them towards their human potential. Einstein was on to this when he said, 'Play is the highest form of research.' He also said, 'The true sign of intelligence is not knowledge but imagination', and I agree that we must move in this direction with education if we are to let our children flourish in this world.

Another way we can help children discover what their heart wants from life is by giving *the arts* the educational standing it deserves. There is this backwards mentality that academic intelligence is the only form of intelligence. Schools judge smart children as those who perform the best academically. Intelligence should not be measured by how much knowledge you can cram into the memory storage centres of your brain from teachers and textbooks. Howard Gardner, in his book, *Frames of Mind - The Theory of Multiple Intelligences*, suggests that there are nine forms of intelligence: naturalist intelligence, musical intelligence, logical-mathematical intelligence, existential intelligence, interpersonal intelligence, bodily-kinaesthetic intelligence, linguistic intelligence, intrapersonal intelligence and spatial intelligence. Although this particular structure is somewhat subjective, it is clear that there are multiple intelligences. If we were to go on Gardner's model of these nine intelligences, I would say there are closer to *ten*. Creative intelligence is another form of intelligence as well. This is measured by a person's ability to invent, whether that be inventing a thought, an idea, a theory, an artwork, a solution or a concept. It is the ability of the brain to create something out of nothing or to build on a previous idea. Progress hinges on this form of intelligence.

Ken Robinson says that public education is based on an out-dated twin-pillar model that nurtures *economic* and *intellectual* ability and not a lot else. In his TED lecture, *Changing Education Paradigms,* Ken says of this model:

My view is that this model has caused chaos in many people's lives. It's been great for some. There have been people who have benefited wonderfully from it - but most people have not.

He goes on further to say that the arts are a victim of this model in a huge way, and I share the same view. Children must be given the opportunity to pursue the arts in the same way they are given the opportunity to pursue intellectual and economic avenues in the current model.

Steiner schools place the arts at the centre of their pedagogy. Otherwise known as Waldorf education, the Steiner method is based on the theory that every human being is an artist. Their mission states:

The program, from nursery through twelfth grade, addresses the physical, emotional and intellectual capacities of the developing child through an age-appropriate curriculum that integrates the disciplines of movement, fine arts, and practical arts into the study of humanities, science, math and technology.

- Steiner.edu/mission

Though I don't agree with the entire approach of the Steiner method, nor do I necessarily agree that every human being is an artist, there is much that can be gleaned from this pedagogy to teaching and the emphasis it places on the arts. I do believe that Rudolf Steiner has moved education in the direction it should be going but there is still much that is missing from this alternative model as well.

The major hurdle that presents itself with the faculty of the arts in public schools is the lack of funding in this department worldwide. Arts programs are being largely ignored financially and there is little monetary incentive for masters of the arts to become teachers in the public school system. As a result of this, when the arts are being taught, the average artisan teacher is under-skilled. If we are to work within this monetary system, we must push for greater funding of arts programs as well as higher salaries for *all* teachers in the public school sector. The only way to get better teachers under the monetary system is to pay them more. Sadly most teachers around the world are on minimum full-time salaries even though their job is as important as those in the highly-paid medical profession. We must recognise the importance of arts programs in helping children to discover their passions and their talents, and start treating the arts with the respect it deserves.

In order to discover what the *self* wants and desires, one must be able to look inwardly for the answer as well. This can be achieved through the practice of **meditation**. Mindfulness has many benefits and there is absolutely no reason why meditation should not be practised in schools. I credit meditation greatly in helping me discover my own path.

*Your visions will become clear only when you can look into your
own heart. Who looks outside, dreams; who looks inside, awakes.*
                                                    - Carl Jung

Meditation allows you to step back from it all; to see the
bigger picture and regain perspective which is often lost. It
establishes a connection with the essence of the *self* and
with the essence of *consciousness*. In this fast-paced world
where our minds are constantly working and our thoughts
are continually on overdrive, we need to be able to take
pause and take stock of life as well. We need time to
remove all our thoughts and clear the mind completely. We
regularly clean out our homes, we get rid of our old clothes
from time to time and we mow the lawns. So why don't
most of us do the same for our minds? They become
convoluted with thoughts, worries and stresses that can
easily lead to physical illnesses. So if there was a way to
uncomplicate the mind and free it from overthinking you
would imagine the entire world would embrace that. Well,
there is a way, through meditation, and it has been
available to us for as long as we have lived on this earth!
Anyone can do it. All you need is a comfortable place to sit
and a spare ten minutes. Of course, the time spent in
meditation varies greatly depending on age and
experience. Beginners can start with 10 minutes a day, and
as you become more experienced with meditation you can
work up to 20 or 30 minutes a day.

The practice of meditation has been known to help
practitioners to achieve a state of inner peace. It is
necessary to be at peace with oneself before one can be a

better person to others. In the world that we live in now, one that is constantly at war with itself and with all living beings, it is crucial that we all start bringing about change in ourselves and try to find peace within ourselves. We can only make things better for everyone else after we make that change in ourselves first.

> *Be the change that you wish to see in the world.*
> - Gandhi

I believe meditation is key to changing oneself. Meditation has a positive effect on the immune system and overall brain health as well. Those who practise mindfulness are less prone to physical illnesses. I got sick four or five times over a seven month period in 2014. Since starting to meditate and de-clutter my mind I have not been sick once. I don't think there has ever been a time when I have gone more than six months without getting sick... that is... until now.

The more consciousness you bring into the body, the stronger the immune system becomes. It is as if every cell awakens and rejoices. The body loves your attention.
> - Eckhart Tolle, *The Power of Now*

To show you these claims have a basis in medical science, I'll refer to several studies conducted on various forms of meditation. One such study conducted by Schneider, Grim & Rainforth et al. looked at 201 men and women with coronary heart disease who took part in one of two groups:

a transcendental meditation (TM) program or a health education program. After 5 and a half years, the TM group showed a 48% risk reduction for heart attack and stroke.

Another study by Pagnoni & Cekic compared grey matter in the brains of Zen meditators and non-meditators over a long period of time. Though grey matter ordinarily reduces with age, the grey matter of the Zen meditators did not reduce at all. In the report, Pagnoni & Cekic stated:

The finding of a reduced rate of decline with age of both global and regional gray matter volume in meditators may in fact indicate the involvement of multiple mechanisms of neuroprotection.

Lazar & Kerr et al. reached a similar conclusion in a study on the impact of meditation on cortical thickness of the brain. They found:

Regular practice of meditation is associated with increased thickness in a subset of cortical regions related to somatosensory, auditory, visual and interoceptive processing. Further, regular meditation practice may slow age-related thinning of the frontal cortex.

Goyal & Singh et al. studied 3515 participants in mindfulness meditation programs and found evidence of decreased anxiety, decreased depression and decreased pain.[2] Indeed, the evidence just keeps mounting that there

---

[2] See *References* for links to all of these scientific studies

are profound health benefits to be gained from meditation practice, and there are no negative effects and no side effects that are often experienced with pharmaceutical drugs.

In his TED talk on meditation, Andy Puddicombe advocates the positive impact the practice can have on life. He refers to meditation as:

...a positive, practical, achievable, scientifically proven technique which allows our mind to be more healthy, to be more mindful and less distracted.

Meditation programs within the educational arena would have significant benefits for children. Not only will kids be able to gain a greater insight into who they are and what drives them, but they will also develop brain neuroplasticity and be healthier, happier and less prone to stress. We should be embracing mindfulness in schools!

There are many different ways of meditating, but meditation in schools need only be about observing the breath. Breathing meditation or Zen meditation is the easiest form of meditation to learn, is extremely effective and does not rely on mantras that may come across to some people as a kind of religious indoctrination. For the record, I am not against mantra meditation, as it is also very effective, but I cannot see it being received well by the general public. The point of meditation in an educational setting is for it not to be an indoctrination, but conversely to be a tool for self-discovery and for heightening conscious awareness. Meditating is about allowing the person to be their *own* teacher. For the youngest children, guided meditation would be a good place to start, and as the children get older, they would move to Zen meditation.

If you're reading this and have no idea how one participates in Zen meditation, or you're eager to start meditating, or perhaps you have tried it before to no avail, here is a quick and easy step-by-step guide:

1. Find a comfortable upright seating position, either cross-legged on a cushion/soft surface or on a soft chair that has good back support.

2. Rest your hands (palms facing outwards) on your knees or in a relaxed position in your lap.

3. Close your eyes and begin to breathe in and out deeply. Focus on the breath as you do so. If any thoughts appear, gently bring the attention back to the breath.

4. Begin to let yourself breathe naturally without forcing the breath. Simply observe your natural breathing. Try not to focus on any sounds you hear. Just observe them coming and going, just like you are observing the breath.

5. Continue to be in the present moment.

If you still struggle to free yourself from your thoughts, do not give up. Like all things in life, keep practising and you will be able to break through that barrier. Perseverance is key. Meditation could very well change your life for the better. It changed mine.

It is so important that we move away from the restricting mentality that education is only about the mind, and recognise that children respond intuitively from the heart.

We live in a left-brain society and a left-brain world. It is a patriarchal society where you do as you're told and you don't ask questions. A left-brain society is one of order, of hierarchy, of little creativity and of little recognition of the aesthetic. It rewards economic productivity and academic achievement but little else. A left-brain society turns humans into machines. It attempts to transform the organic into the inorganic, which is counterintuitive to our human nature. Conversely, the right-brain is about creativity, sensuality and randomness. Of course, if we had a right-brain society exclusively there would be no structure at all, and our society would not function effectively.

There must be a balance between the left-brain and the right-brain in any society. There is a reason we have a left hemisphere and a right hemisphere in our brain that perform opposing functions. They are there to complement each other. They are there to maintain equilibrium. Just like men are here to complement women and women are here to complement men. Without the existence of inverses, nothing could exist. Newton's third law of motion states that *for every reaction there is an equal and opposite reaction.*

The Chinese say that life is all about the *yin* and the *yang*.
They are opposite in nature yet they complement one
another. To continue along this line of thinking, the *yin* and
the *yang* are completely out of balance in our education
system, and there is an urgent need to restore that balance.
We can only do that by giving right-brain learners the same
opportunities we give to left-brain learners. We need to
give *all* children access to the tools and resources necessary
to discover their innermost passions and help them wake
up to what is inside of them...

In a properly automated and educated world, machines may prove to be the true humanizing influence. It may be that machines will do the work that makes life possible and that human beings will do all the other things that make life pleasant and worthwhile.

Isaac Asimov

A Brave New World

First there was fire. Then came the wheel, the printing press, the steam engine, the telephone, the computer, the television, the inkjet printer, the mobile phone, the world wide web, the digital revolution, and now the emergence of artificial intelligence. We have come a long way since the stone age and technological growth is not showing any signs of slowing down.

Right now we are entering a new technological age. This is the age of automation - the rise of the machines. We now have machines that are capable of printing three-dimensional objects. 3D printing technology is capable of printing anything from toys to clothing to car parts and even prosthetics.

The D-Shape Printer, invented by Enrico Dini in Italy, uses sand and a magnesium-based binding agent to print entire one and two storey buildings that have a texture not dissimilar to concrete. Joris Laarman has created a freely-moving robot arm that 3D prints large objects using metal pixels he calls 'voxels'. Dr. Anthony Atala has succeeded in printing human organs that he combines with cells from the patient to bring those newly printed organs to life. This has far-reaching implications for the medical field.

The printer that has my attention is far simpler than all of these printers. It is called the RepRap, short for replicating rapid prototyper, and it was invented by Adrian Bowyer from the UK. What separates the RepRap from the rest of the 3D printing world is that it has the ability to print most of its own parts, as well as the ability to print household objects, and costs only $500 (US). The parts of itself that the RepRap cannot print are widely available worldwide and cost next-to-nothing. Not only this, but the RepRap project is open-source, meaning that it is free for anyone to build upon and improve. The RepRap project is therefore likely to move along in leaps and bounds, and the parts of itself it will be able to print will be likely to increase more and more in the coming years. The RepRap community hopes that the printer will soon be able to print all of its own parts.

Just think about it. A person can have one of these in their garage, and print another one. They can then print two more, which can print four more and so on... all at zero cost! Then seven potential friends/relatives of that person can have their own RepRap that can print more RepRaps. The RepRap has the potential to reduce poverty on a global scale, as it would eliminate the need to buy basic material items if everyone had one in their home. Entire industries would become obsolete and corporations would tumble like a house of cards. There would be no need for department stores and no need for many trade industries. This is not an exaggeration. The sheer potential of the self-replicating function of the RepRap poses a very serious threat to the capitalist model, and the RepRap is only in its infancy. I'll come back to this a bit later.

Science and technology have made incredible progress in other areas of robotics as well. The Kiva Systems robot, created by Mick Mountz, locates warehouse items and brings them to the front of the warehouse. It does this by lifting up a whole warehouse shelf, called a pod, and transporting that pod to the front for a 'picker' employee to retrieve the desired item from the pod. As this is happening, hundreds of other Kiva robots are transporting pods as well. Instead of crashing into each other, the robots are programmed to navigate around each other with a 100% success rate. It's very hard for me to describe this process. You need to see it for yourself. You can find videos of the Kiva robot in action on YouTube. Mountz's company, Kiva Systems, was purchased by Amazon.com in 2012 for $775 million.

The SaviOne robot, by robotics company Savioke, is the world's first fully-operational butler robot. The SaviOne, or Botlr as it has been affectionately named, is currently up and running in the Aloft Cupertino Hotel, California. When a hotel patron asks for room service, the clerk at the front desk places the item inside Botlr's top-storage compartment and the robot makes the journey to the specific room number of the patron, before alerting the patron that their item has arrived. Botlr even knows how to use the elevator! Service robots like these could have applications throughout the entire service industry. If the SaviOne is anything to go by, there will eventually be robots that take your order at a restaurant and bring that order to the table when it's ready.

DASH, short for Dynamic Autonomous Sprawled Hexapod, is a 10cm long robot with insect-like legs, that is capable of running at high speeds and surviving incredibly high falls. It can even climb obstacles taller than its height. It is hoped that DASH will eventually be used in natural disaster situations in locating people in need of assistance.

Of course, we all know that some robots are not being used for benevolent means. Drones are remote-controlled aircrafts of varying shapes and sizes that are being used by the American and Israeli military to kill people. They also assist in spying and reconnaissance missions for intelligence agencies, but their primary directive is *shoot to kill*. Predator drones are equipped with highly destructive weaponry, and US drone strikes have already killed thousands of people, including hundreds of civilians.

Boston Dynamics, a military robotics developer, has been working on a series of intimidating-looking machines that have various uses for the US army. First, there is BigDog, which looks just like that, a big dog, except it doesn't have a head. Instead, it has a robotic arm where the head should be. I needn't tell you how unsettling that image must be. BigDog, as far as we have been shown, is capable of manoeuvring across difficult terrain, carrying heavy supplies, and hurling giant cinderblocks far across a room. Then there's Cheetah, another beast-sized robot which can run faster than a human being. There is also

PetMan, a humanoid that walks and moves similarly to us. Put a camo suit on him and you can't tell the difference between PetMan and a human being. Finally, there's Sand Flea, a tiny four-wheeler that can leap up to 30 feet in the air in any direction and can withstand the impact from large falls! Boston Dynamics, along with eight other robotics companies, was purchased in 2013 by Google. Yes, you are reading that right. For some reason, your favourite search engine owns an army of intelligent, potentially-killer robots. Since the acquisition of these companies by Google, news of further developments in these robots has been 'hush-hush' and the media have not even been given as much as a sniff. A comforting thought indeed, considering Google's omnipresence in our lives.

On the one hand, drones and other killer robots present a potentially grim and dystopian future; one in which humans use machines to maintain dominance over other humans. This is an outcome that 99% of us do not want, and it is up to us to ensure that we do not head down this road. On the other hand, machines have the potential to make life better for all human beings. We do not need to fear the machines. Provided we use them to assist rather than to harm, they could be the best thing to happen to humans in thousands of years.

Do a quick search on the internet and you'll find hundreds of articles about machines replacing the jobs of humans. It seems that no matter where you look, people are concerned about technological unemployment. Yes, machines are replacing humans in the workforce, and fast. This is a *good* thing! If we get rid of the monetary system, machines could do all those jobs that humans don't want to. In fact, the rise of automation is detrimental to the monetary system. Capitalism is not just shooting itself in the foot, it is shooting itself in the foot and letting itself bleed to death. On the surface, replacing human workers with machines that are more efficient seems like a great thing for company productivity. However, higher unemployment means less consumption. Less consumption means a worse economy. Under the current monetary system, machines are counter-intuitive to growth.

But if we got rid of money, that would be flipped on its head. We could have machines doing all those unpleasant, soulless jobs, while we focus our attention on what really drives us as human beings. It could be playing music, creating art, travelling with our families, innovating new technologies, or even solving the mysteries of the universe and ancient civilisations! We could have a RepRap in every home that could print out recyclable objects for domestic use, and an automated garbage disposal/recycling system. We could have robots to assist us in every walk of life. Money would no longer serve a purpose. Guy Rundle speaks about the potential impact automation could have on the system in his book, *A Revolution in the Making*:

The exponential spread of such machines would make the capitalist markets for a wide range of goods unsustainable, and capitalism would collapse of its own accord.

Under an Ubuntu system, which I will come to in chapter 9, no human being would be allowed to suffer and people would contribute their talents and passions for the good of the community. I believe this to be the way forward.

Think about the kinds of technological breakthroughs we could make without the bureaucratic red tape that goes along with profit-based growth. If we open-sourced all our ideas in a moneyless world we would progress tenfold the rate we are now. We only need to take a leaf from the book of a person like Doug Coulter to see what we could achieve in such a world. Doug is just an ordinary guy living in a backwoods cabin in Virginia in the US, who has had a degree of success developing a nuclear fusion reactor in his workshop. He has open-sourced all of his work and made it available to a whole community of passionate freelance scientists who he is in constant contact with over the internet. Doug has probably come the closest to cracking nuclear fusion of anyone in history, and his work still continues. Nuclear fusion power provides us with a source of renewable energy that could power every country in the world. In a documentary on Coulter's work by Motherboard, a successful YouTube channel dedicated to future technology and innovation, Doug says:

Big science has been failing at this miserably. They aren't able to do anything quickly. Everything is meetings and bureaucracy. Here, it's just, can I make fusion work? No one's getting in my way. I'm not getting in anyone else's way. It's me against the universe!

MagLev technology (or magnetic levitation technology) is another area that has incredible potential. MagLev trains are now being developed in a handful of countries around the world, with trains in Japan and China already fully operational. The Japanese MagLev train is the fastest train in the world, capable of speeds exceeding 580 km/h. MagLev trains do not have the need for wheels or an internal engine. They are run entirely by electromagnetism. The train never touches the track. It is suspended in the air a number of centimetres above the track, meaning that friction is not a factor. Without surface friction, MagLev trains are able to exceed the velocity of high-speed-rail trains by hundreds of kilometres per hour. That being said, the speeds that the MagLev trains are reaching now are nothing compared to what is possible with this technology. Air resistance is currently holding back the MagLev train from reaching its full potential.

Enter 'evacuated tube transport'. This is where things get really interesting. Evacuated tube transport is a revolutionary transport system whereby MagLev train pods travel through a vacuum inside a tube. As there is zero air resistance inside a vacuum, MagLev trains can reach speeds of up to 6500 kilometres per hour! That's New York to Beijing in 2 hours... and this technology is just inside of our grasp.

Daryl Oster, the CEO at ET3, was the first to take the idea seriously and his company is working on making it a reality. Instead of electromagnetic suspension (EMS), these 'super-maglevs' operate using electrodynamic suspension (EDS), which utilises a superconductor and liquid nitrogen to keep the train suspended. If that sounds 'out there', bear with me.

A group of researchers at Tel-Aviv University, led by Boaz Almog, discovered this phenomenon. It is known as quantum levitation or quantum locking. In 2012, Boaz stunned a large audience at The UP Experience Forum in Houston, Texas, when he demonstrated quantum levitation in action. In the demonstration video, he takes a small round disc made out of sapphire crystal and a hard superconducting material. He then submerges the disc in a solution of freezing-cold liquid nitrogen. With a pair of tweezers he removes the disc and places it in the empty space above a magnet. Lo and behold, the disc levitates in the air, locked inside the magnetic field being generated. He tilts the disc on its side, and it remains in that position, as if time itself has been frozen. No matter what position the disc is manipulated into, it stays locked in that position until he moves it again. Even when the magnet is tipped upside down so that the disc is between the magnet and the ground, gravity still does not affect the disc and it does not fall to the ground. This goes against everything mainstream physics has stood by for centuries. Then Boaz takes it a step further. He suspends the disc above a circular magnetic track and gives it a push. It hovers effortlessly along the track like Marty McFly's hover-board in *Back to the Future*. Then he places the disc on the underside of the track, gives it a push, and it hovers in the space underneath the track. Who needs gravity anyway, right?

The quantum world holds the key to both our advancement in the field of science and technology as well as our understanding of the mysteries of consciousness. I'll revisit this in chapter 8. The reason why I've covered this content in this chapter is twofold. First of all, it's important that people know the direction we are heading and our innovative potential as a human race... and more importantly, science in our education system is due for an overhaul - a paradigm shift. Science education must start to look more closely at quantum physics and quantum mechanics, and must break free of the rigidity that has kept it so boxed-in and constrained. We have to stop putting everything in boxes and open our minds to the mentality that 'there is no box'. I am a strong advocate for science, but we need to accept that we don't know nearly as much as we think we do about the way the universe works. The scientific pursuit of knowledge is a never-ending pursuit, for the universe is likely infinite in itself. We will never stop discovering more. It is for this reason that we cannot profess to know all the principles of science, and must not allow ourselves to be locked in this way.

We are stepping into a new frontier of advanced technology and opening up breakthrough possibilities in the realm of quantum physics. Our global society needs to let go of its rigid paradigms that do nothing but hold back our progress as a human race. Change is necessary in order to grow. We must have the wisdom to adapt to the changing world around us and the courage to venture boldly into the unknown...

There is geometry in the humming of the strings.
There is music in the spacing of the spheres.

Pythagoras

The Geometric Code

Mathematics is also due for a paradigm shift in schools. We should be teaching our children the sacred geometrical knowledge of our ancestors. Don't let the word *sacred* fool you into thinking this has anything to do with religion. Anyone who associates this knowledge with worship is missing the point altogether. *Sacred geometry* refers to the mathematical knowledge held by ancient civilizations and makes up the very building blocks of nature. If the word *sacred* is bothersome, and I can understand why, perhaps think of it as *existential geometry* or *cosmological geometry* (termed *cosmometry*). It is often referred to as *the architecture of life* and offers a completely transformative way of looking at mathematics, and of looking at life itself. There is sacred geometry in everything from the proportions of living organisms to ancient buildings and even music. Its beauty is in its simplicity. From the most basic two-dimensional shape, the circle, we can find an entire set of informational systems that give us a profound insight into the language of the universe and the existence of everything in our natural world. I would like to share the foundations of this knowledge with you, as I have understood it, so as to demonstrate its educational merit. If this does not interest you, feel free to move on to the next chapter. I assure you that if you stay with me you should find much of this information eye-opening and it may provide you with a new perspective, should this knowledge resonate with you.

We begin with a perfect circle (Figure 1a). From the very top of this circle, we create another circle of the same radius, such that the centre of each circle lies on the perimeter of the other. The area where the two circles intersect is called the *vesica piscis*. You can see this in the shaded region of Figure 1b.

Figure 1a: A perfect circle.

Figure 1b: A second intersecting circle. The *vesica piscis* is indicated by the shaded region.

The vesica piscis can be found in many places, from the human eye to the hourglass nebula in the cosmos.

There is a great deal of mathematical information contained within the vesica piscis, such as the square roots of 2, 3, and 5 (all infinitely recurring numbers), but I'm going to move on from this shape for now. Next, we create a third circle of the same radius so that its centre point is aligned with point A (Figure 1c).

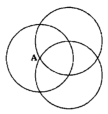

Figure 1c: A third intersecting circle with centre point *A*.

This circle should also pass through the centre points of both the first two circles. From this pattern, we derive both the symbol of the *trinity* and the *equilateral triangle* (Figure 1d).

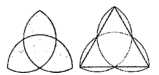

Figure 1d: The *trinity* symbol and *equilateral triangle* derived from the three circles.

We create a fourth circle so that its centre aligns with point B (Figure 1e overleaf). Continuing in this pattern, we keep creating circles until there are a total of seven circles including the original. The resulting pattern is called the *seed of life*[3] (Figure 1f). From this we can derive two perfect hexagons, one rotated inside another (Figure 1g).

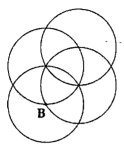

Figure 1e: A fourth circle with centre point *B*.

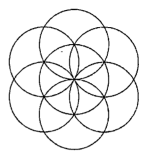

Figure 1f: The *seed of life* pattern.

Figure 1g: Connecting the points in this way gives us two perfect hexagons.

We then create another layer of circles using the same rule as before (placing the circles at each intersecting node), giving us twelve new circles (Figure 1h opposite). Hidden

---

[3] Please note that the names of these patterns I am describing are only the *popular* labels for them. I am using these labels as I find them easiest to distinguish between. The names don't really matter.

within this new design there is a three-dimensional shape known as the *egg of life* (Figure 2a).

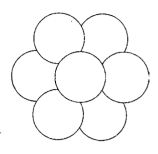

Figure 1h: Another outer layer of 12 new circles.

Figure 2a: The *egg of life* pattern.

This structure can be found in the human embryo in the first few hours of creation (Figure 2b).

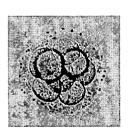

Figure 2b: The human embryo in the first few hours of creation.

Figure 2c: The *flower of life* pattern.

Now let's see what we find when we create yet another layer of circles around the outside of the extended seed of life pattern. Eighteen circles later and we have another pattern called the *flower of life* (Figure 2c). This pattern is of special significance as it has been discovered by historians and archaeologists all over the ancient world. The flower of life pattern has been found inscribed on a wall with ochre stain at the Temple of Osiris in Abydos, Egypt (Figure 2d) with stunning accuracy.

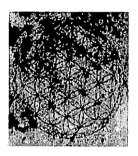

Figure 2d: The inscription at the
Temple of Osiris in Abydos, Egypt.

It is also hidden very cleverly on a ball underneath the paw of one of the guardian lions at the Imperial Palace of the Forbidden City in Beijing, China (Figure 2e).

Figure 2e: The *flower of life* pattern at
the Imperial Palace of the Forbidden
City in Beijing, China.

Figure 2f: The *flower of life* mosaic
in Ephesus, Turkey.

The flower of life pattern has also been spotted as a mosaic in Ephesus, Turkey, and outside the Golden Temple in Amritsar, India (Figures 2f, and 2g).

Figure 2g: The *flower of life* pattern outside the Golden Temple in Amritsar, India.

Even Leonardo Da Vinci had knowledge of this pattern, as evidenced in his drawings within the Codex Atlanticus (Figure 2h).

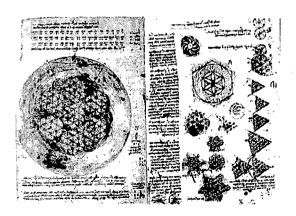

Figure 2h: Da Vinci's drawings in the *Codex Atlanticus.*

Let's continue to build on this pattern with one final outer layer of circles (Figure 3a). We then remove all but 13 circles of this new pattern, and we are left with another symbol called the *fruit of life* (Figure 3b).

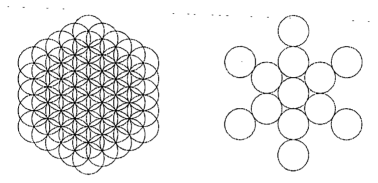

Figure 3a: A final outer layer of circles.

Figure 3b: Removing all but 13 circles gives us this pattern called the *fruit of life*.

What is the meaning of this cluster of circles? When we draw a straight line connecting the centre of each circle to the centre of every other circle, we get a three-dimensional shape known as *Metatron's cube* (Figure 3c).

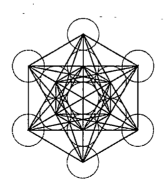

Figure 3c: *Metatron's Cube.*

From this mysterious shape we can easily derive four of the five *Platonic solids*. Plato claimed that these five solids are the building blocks of everything in existence, both organic and inorganic. These are very unique three-dimensional polyhedra, as they are the only solids that have the same shaped faces and the same number of faces meeting at all vertices. The four Platonic solids that can be easily derived are the *tetrahedron*, the *hexahedron* (or cube), the *octahedron* and the *dodecahedron*. The *icosahedron* (Plato's fifth solid) requires slightly more information to derive an accurate representation from Metatron's cube, but that would be getting into more advanced geometric concepts that I don't need to cover. In Figure 3d you can see how these four Platonic solids are derived from Metatron's cube.

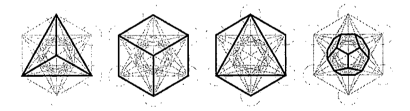

Figure 3d: Finding four of the *Platonic Solids* in *Metatron's Cube*. In order: The *tetrahedron*, the *hexahedron* (or cube), the *octahedron* and the *dodecahedron*.

Also hidden in Metatron's cube is a 2D representation of another three-dimensional solid called the *star tetrahedron*. The star tetrahedron is formed by two tetrahedra inverted within one another (Figure 3e overleaf).

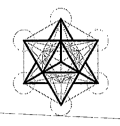

Figure 3e: The *star tetrahedron*
found in *Metatron's Cube.*

Now let's take a look at a shape everyone is familiar with:
the *regular pentagon* (Figure 3f). The US Department of
Defense constructed and named their headquarters based
on this very shape, and you'll see a couple of possible
reasons why in a moment. If we draw straight lines
connecting all the vertices of the pentagon, we get another
shape known as the *pentagram* (Figure 3g). In the centre of
the pentagram we find another perfect pentagon, albeit
inverted.

Figure 3f: A regular pentagon. **Figure 3g:** Connecting all the vertices
gives us the *pentagram.*

When we connect the vertices again with straight lines we
get another pentagram. With the help of these connecting
lines, the pentagram can therefore be repeated inside itself
an infinite amount of times (Figure 3h).

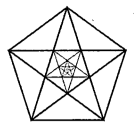

Figure 3h: The *pentagram* can reproduce itself an infinite amount of times.

Some of you may know the pentagram as a shape associated with certain secret societies and occultist beliefs, but there is actually a very important mathematical code hidden in the lines of the pentagram. This is a code known as the *golden ratio*, or *phi (φ)*. Figure 4a shows the phi (φ) ratio marked on a straight line where **a + b is to a** as **a is to b**. Take a moment to look at this diagram to get an idea of the proportions of this ratio.

Figure 4a: The *golden ratio* represented on a straight line.

The golden ratio is *approximately* equal to 1.618. Now when we look closely at the diagram of the pentagram in Figure 4b overleaf we can see the golden ratio represented in three different ways, where $\frac{a}{b} = φ$, $\frac{b}{c} = φ$, and $\frac{c}{d} = φ$. To me, that is something quite remarkable in itself!

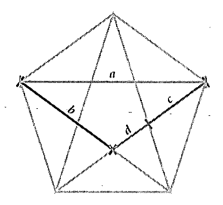

Figure 4b: The *pentagram* contains
the *golden ratio* three times.

Using this same principle, we can create what is known as
the *golden rectangle* (Figure 4c). This is a rectangle where the
ratio of the length 'a' to the width 'b' is equal to phi (φ).

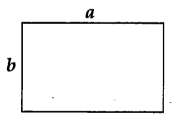

Figure 4c: A *golden rectangle*.

The golden rectangle can reproduce smaller and smaller
versions of itself to infinity, and we can show the
relationship between each of these golden rectangles with a
Golden Mean Spiral (Figure 4d opposite). The Golden Mean
Spiral has no beginning and no end, which gives it a rather

mesmerising quality. I'll revisit this golden spiral in a moment.

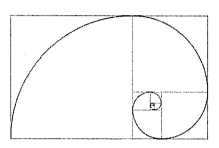

Figure 4d: *A golden mean spiral.*

During the 12th century, a man named Leonardo Pisano came up with a sequence of numbers known as the Fibonacci sequence. Consequently, Pisano became known to the world as Fibonacci. The Fibonacci sequence is a series of numbers in which each progressive number is equal to the sum of the two preceding numbers. The first ten numbers of the Fibonacci sequence are 1, 1, 2, 3, 5, 8, 13, 21, 34, 55. Here, you can see that 1 + 2 = 3, 2 + 3 = 5, 5 + 8 = 13 and so on. The number 1 appears twice, as 0 would technically precede the sequence, and we know 0 + 1 = 1. One of the reasons the Fibonacci sequence is so significant is because it is extremely closely related to the golden ratio, phi (φ). If we divide the second number by the first ($\frac{1}{1}$) we are of course left with the ratio of 1. However, divide the fifth number by the fourth ($\frac{5}{3}$) and we get approximately 1.67, a completely different ratio. The next ratio we find ($\frac{8}{5}$) gives us exactly 1.6. Do you see what's happening as we progress through the Fibonacci sequence? The ratio seems to be getting closer and closer to φ (approx. 1.618). When we take two neighbouring numbers from the high end of the sequence, for instance $\frac{6765}{4181}$, we get a ratio so incredibly close to **phi** that it only differs after the first seven decimal places. The higher the Fibonacci sequence goes, the closer it gets to **phi**... but it *never* quite gets there. You can see this relationship as a waveform in Figure 4e. Notice how the Fibonacci ratios alternate between moving above and below the **phi** line as they progress. This relationship is so closely bonded that when you map a Fibonacci spiral it looks very much like the golden mean spiral (Figure 4f opposite). The biggest difference between the two is that the Fibonacci spiral has a beginning (at the number 1), whereas the golden mean spiral does not. So what's the significance of all of this? Well, if we look at the world around us, we see that the Fibonacci sequence is encoded all throughout nature.

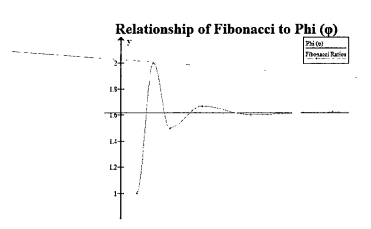

Figure 4e: Waveform relationship between *Fibonacci* and *Phi.*

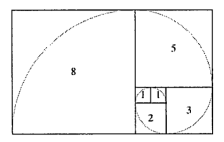

Figure 4f: A *Fibonacci spiral*. The numbers indicate the length of the squares based on the Fibonacci sequence.

We see it in the branches of plants and trees, in the seeds of a sunflower, in the rind of a pineapple, in leaves, pinecones and strawberries! We find Fibonacci spirals in the shape of the human ear, in far-away galaxies, in the nautilus shell and many other places. The fact that this code is embedded all over the place still baffles people to this day, and has many theorising that the universe may be fractal-holographic in nature.

The fractal-holographic view of the universe suggests that all forms of matter are really just a blur of interference patterns that our brain decodes into physical reality. The *fractal* nature of this theory takes into account the repetition of patterns at all scales. For example, if you look at an image of the neuronal structure in the brain and compare it to an image scientists have constructed of the universe you will see a striking similarity, so much so that it may call into question your entire view of existence. The *holographic* nature of this theory suggests that what we think of as the material world is just a projection.

There is evidence to suggest that our world and everything in it –
from snowflakes to maple trees to falling stars and spinning
electrons – are also only ghostly images, projections from a level
of reality so beyond our own it is literally beyond both space and
time.

- Michael Talbot, *The Holographic Universe*

Of course, no one can be absolutely 100% certain whether
or not the universe is a hologram at this stage, but the field
of quantum physics is rapidly providing compelling
evidence that gives credence to this explanation. I will be
revisiting the quantum world in Chapter 8.

Getting back to the topic at hand, we see **phi (φ)** in the
bone structures and proportions of animals, including
humans. They have become known as the *golden*
proportions. Features of the human body that are in golden
proportion to one another appear to be the most
aesthetically pleasing. The bones of the average human
index finger are in golden proportion to one another. Note
how I said *average*, as this is not the case for everyone,
myself included! It is merely the benchmark for physical
perfection in nature and in living organisms. Leonardo Da
Vinci incorporated these golden proportions into most of
his artworks, including his most famous work, *The Mona*
Lisa.

The ancients were well aware of this geometrical
marvel. The ancient Greeks had very strict guidelines for
their buildings and statues, and insisted in **phi (φ)** being
integral to their design. It can be seen all throughout their
architecture, from the Parthenon to the Statue of Adonis.

Though the identity of the chief architect of the Taj Mahal mausoleum in India is largely unconfirmed (it is widely *believed* to be a Persian by the name of Ustad Ahmad Lahauri), whoever designed this majestic tomb did so with great attention to the golden ratio. We find many golden rectangles present in the construction of this wonder of the world.

Even all the way back as far as ancient Egypt we see signs that these geometrical principles were adhered to. The Great Pyramid of Giza exhibits an extremely close representation of **phi** (with an error of only 0.025%) in the ratio of the apothem to half the base. This would have had to be an extraordinary coincidence for this to be achieved by accident, and the evidence reveals that the builders of these pyramids (whoever they were) were highly intelligent and possessed advanced knowledge of the stars.

Graham Hancock, an author and journalist who researched the significance of the Pyramids of Giza for many years, conducting much of his research on site, discovered that the three main pyramids are a mirrored representation of the three stars of Orion's belt. Not only this, but he also found that tiny shafts leading out of the Great Pyramid pointed directly at specific constellations in the sky. One such shaft, leading out from the room known as the 'Queen's Chamber', pointed directly at the star, Sirius, which he said was identified by ancient Egyptians with the figure, Isis. He found that the King's Chamber had another shaft that pointed directly at the stars of Orion's belt, and it was known that Orion was associated with the Egyptian figure, Osiris. You can see the scientific process behind Hancock's revelations in his ground-breaking three-part documentary, *Quest for the Lost Civilization* (1998). Whoever built the Pyramids of Giza did so in a highly calculated way and I am certain the golden ratio was used as a guide for the construction of the Great Pyramid.

Michael Tellinger, explorer, writer and the visionary behind the Ubuntu Contributionism model that I will be coming to in chapter 9, pioneered research into the ancient stone circle ruins of South Africa as well as a fascinating site known now as Adam's Calendar. He and fellow researcher Johan Heine discovered that many of the ancient stone structures (of which there have been more than a million recorded throughout the South African countryside), were built in accordance with advanced geometrical alignments. There is a growing body of geological evidence suggesting that these structures were built over 100,000 years ago. Adam's Calendar is a hugely important site, near the southern-most tip of South Africa in the Mpumalanga Province, that has been left out of the history books. Through his analysis of the man-made stone monoliths of the Adam's Calendar site, Tellinger has produced evidence that the site is around 75,000 years old. He believes it to be the real birthplace of homo sapiens. Though this is a startling claim, I highly recommend you look closely at Tellinger's research as it is not to be scoffed at.

Since he lifted the lid on this ancient site many more scientists and researchers have expressed a real interest in it. Currently, the site has been closed off by the South

African authorities and Tellinger is having a hard time accessing it. Why would they close this site off to scientists and researchers, who have a genuine interest in preserving the site, unless Tellinger was really on to something? Take into consideration that the authorities only closed this site after Tellinger had made its existence public. If the site was just a bunch of rocks and didn't have any historical meaning at all, there would be absolutely no reason to close it off. To further substantiate the significance of this site, there is a stone carved into the form of the Egyptian figure, Horus, and another stone carved into the form of an Egyptian Sphinx. Tellinger found these stones to predate the ancient Egyptian age by tens of thousands of years, suggesting that there is much more to our history than we are led to believe through the conventional history books.

Adding to this mystery, the Adam's Calendar site, which is on the edge of a cliff, looks down at a small cluster of very distinct pyramids that share a resemblance to the pyramids at Giza. While Michael Tellinger was trying to understand the meaning of these pyramids beneath the Adam's Calendar site, he had an amazing revelation. Superimposing a Golden Mean Spiral over the top of a map of this region of the Mpumalanga Province, he found that the Adam's Calendar site and the pyramids below both aligned perfectly with the golden spiral. For this to have been a complete coincidence, the odds would have been millions to one. Tellinger displays the visual proof of this in his compelling presentation, *Ancient Technology and the Ubuntu Movement*, that was part of the Breakthrough Energy Movement forum in 2012. You can find this presentation on YouTube. Tellinger also explains that the pyramids at Adam's Calendar line up perfectly with both the ruins of Great Zimbabwe (which Tellinger contends were built by the same hands as whoever built Adam's Calendar) and the Great Pyramid of Giza along the 31 Degrees East Longitudinal line! Again, he demonstrates this in his presentation. This discovery has proven that the pyramids of Egypt at the northern end of the continent are connected with the Adam's Calendar site at the southern end of the continent, which leads us to believe that the Giza pyramids may be much older than we thought.

Not only is geometry a key piece of the puzzle in decoding the mysteries of the ancient world, but it is also much more important to our understanding of the nature of the universe than conventional wisdom has accepted for many centuries. Just look at the science of *cymatics*. If you haven't heard of cymatics before, it's the process of examining the visible form of soundwave vibration. All sound frequencies produce a specific vibration, and when these vibrations are targeted through various forms of matter, the physical particles of the matter organise themselves into different shapes and patterns, dependent on the sound frequency. For example, experiments have been conducted using grains of sand on a metal plate hooked up to a sound frequency generator. As the sound comes out of the generator, the metal plate vibrates and the sand organises itself into various shapes based on the vibrational frequency (Figure 4g opposite).

Figure 4g: Sand organising itself into various patterns based on the vibrational frequencies of sound.

Others have produced the same effect by running a violin bow across the edge of the metal plate. There are plenty of videos on YouTube to prove the existence of this phenomenon. You really do need to see it with your own eyes to get a sense of how mind-blowing it is. Experiments have also been conducted using water as a medium for sound vibrations. In this case, it is the way in which the water ripples outwards due to the sound frequency that produces different effects. Figure 4h shows the recognisable geometric shapes in the rippling of water that is being manipulated by these soundwaves.

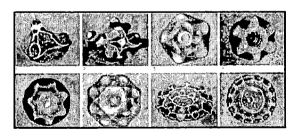

Figure 4h: Various rippling effects of water based on sound vibration.

The study of cymatics has opened up the possibility for sound being converted into a source of free energy. A team at the Queen Mary University of London, led by Dr. Steve

Dunn, is researching how to do this, and has so far had success at the nano-scale. This is an amazing breakthrough, and if it could be scaled up, the benefits for society would be enormous. A man by the name of Peter Davey invented a device in 2008 that he claimed could boil water using the vibrational energy of sound. He came up with the idea when he noticed that different household objects would vibrate when he played different notes on his saxophone.

Unfortunately, Davey chose to keep the knowledge of his invention to himself, while waiting for the right investor, and he died before he could cash in on it. Had he open-sourced his invention to the world, we would probably have been able to convert sound energy on a larger scale by now.

Geometry may also be a key component in unlocking the potential of what is called zero-point energy. Zero-point energy refers to the energy contained inside a vacuum. Nikola Tesla spent much of his life trying to understand and harness this form of energy, which he referred to as the energy of the aether. In the closing remarks of a lecture to the American Institute of Electrical Engineers at Columbia College in May of 1891, Tesla stated of the potential contained in the zero-point energy field:

We are whirling through endless space with an inconceivable speed, all around us everything is spinning, everything is moving, everywhere is energy. There must be some way of availing ourselves of this energy more directly. Then, with the light obtained from the medium, with the power derived from it, with every form of energy obtained without effort, from the store forever inexhaustible, humanity will advance with great strides.

Nikola Tesla understood how to extract the energy from the vacuum and turn it into electricity, but developments in this area of his research were thwarted by his major financier, banker John Pierpont Morgan, who refused to continue to fund Tesla's projects. Many say J.P. Morgan, who held the monopoly over the lucrative copper-wire energy industry at the time, cut off Tesla's funding in fear of not being able to make a profit from this energy.

Morgan is quoted as saying, 'If anyone can draw on the power, where do we put the meter?' In her book, *Tesla: Man Out of Time*, Margaret Cheney explains that Tesla did not disclose to Morgan the full extent of his plans with regard to the use of the funding, and only told Morgan about his ideas for global telegraphic communication. Of course, Tesla's real goal was to achieve the wireless transmission of electricity.

Cheney writes of the initial letter Tesla penned to J.P. Morgan requesting funding for his projects:

He made no mention to Morgan of the wireless transmission of power, not because he had given up the idea, but for the prudent reason that it would have made some of the banker's existing investments obsolete. In any event Mr. Morgan could not be expected to be enthusiastic about the prospect of beaming electricity to penniless Zulus or Pygmies.

Tesla went to his grave not having realised his goal of free energy for everyone, as he was thrown into a significant debt. Now, it seems, the world is waking up to the true genius of Nikola Tesla and many have been inspired by his work with zero-point energy. Two Russian brothers, Leonid and Sergey Plekhanov have plans to re-engineer Tesla's Wardenclyffe Tower. Tesla originally built this tower in 1901 to transmit electricity wirelessly, and Margaret Cheney writes that huge bolts of lightning were witnessed by onlookers when Tesla activated the giant coil atop the tower. Tesla's financial situation meant that his plans for the tower were never fully realised and the site was shut down. The Plekhanov brothers, both avid physicists, are currently in the process of rebuilding this great tower. You can follow their progress at the project's website: *globalenergytransmission.com*.

A man by the name of Buckminster Fuller, most well-known for the geodesic dome structure he created in the 1940s, is perhaps less well-known for discovering the geometry of the vacuum. In other words, he found the underlying geometric system of the zero-point energy field! He called it the *vector equilibrium* (Figure 5a opposite). Fuller found that it was the only three-dimensional shape in which all of the vectors, both radial and circumferential, were of equal length. The forces of the radial vectors (shown by the edges in Figure 5a coming out from the centre point) precisely counterbalanced the forces of the circumferential vectors (the edges around the outside). The forces were said to be in perfect equilibrium and thus represented a condition of complete stillness; the *zerophase*.

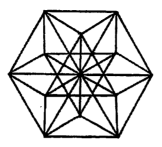

Figure 5a: The *vector equilibrium.*

'Bucky', as he was known, said that this was the state in which all forms emerged. He called it the 'starting point'.

In his book, *Synergetics*, Fuller wrote:

The vector equilibrium is the minimum operational model of happenings... it is the empty theatre and empty universe intercoordinatingly ready to accommodate any act and any audience.

Bucky found that the vector equilibrium could be extended outwards seeing as all the vectors were entirely balanced. This produced a geometric grid he called the *isotropic vector matrix* (Figure 5b overleaf). The grid was made up of interconnecting tetrahedra (triangular pyramids).

Nassim Haramein, researcher and quantum physicist, found inspiration in Buckminster Fuller's work and sought to continue it. He looked closely at the structure of the isotropic vector matrix and found that there were negative cavities inside that matrix which caused asymmetry.

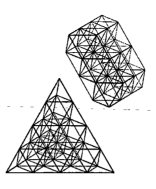

Figure 5b: Fuller's *Isotropic Vector Matrix.*

IMAGE CREDIT: Buckminster Fuller.

In other words, he found that in the middle of the isotropic vector matrix were tetrahedra that did not share the same properties as all of the other tetrahedra in the grid; they were *rotated* away from the other tetrahedra. When he noticed this asymmetry, he realised that there was an imbalance of positive and negative polarities inside the structure. So Haramein set to work, and eventually came up with what he believed to be the solution - a structure he called the *64 tetrahedron grid* (Figure 5c opposite).

In this structure are 32 tetrahedra pointing *up* and 32 tetrahedra pointing *down*. This indicates completely balanced polarities. On further examining the 64 tetrahedron grid, we can see that it is actually made up of a large star tetrahedron (two tetrahedra inversely placed inside one another) and a large vector equilibrium. You can see the large vector equilibrium more clearly in Figure 5d opposite.

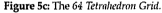

Figure 5c: The *64 Tetrahedron Grid.*

Figure 5d: The *64 Tetrahedron Grid* represented as a solid.

IMAGE CREDIT: Nassim Haramein.

Nassim Haramein also came to the realisation that the star tetrahedron was made up of 8 smaller tetrahedra pointing *out* and the vector equilibrium was made up of 8 tetrahedra pointing *in*. Again, proof of perfectly balanced polarities and perfect equilibrium in one perfect structure! If you are scratching your head at all, I highly recommend Haramein's video presentation titled *Crossing the Event Horizon*. It's quite lengthy, but I can assure you it is time very well spent, and he explains it all so well. Haramein is now part of a quantum physics think-tank he helped create called *The Resonance Project,* which is dedicated to proving the universal field theory and finding practical applications for it in the world. If you would like to find out more about The Resonance Project, their website is *resonance.is.*

If Haramein's project is successful, humanity may be looking at evolutionary technologies very soon that do not appear to abide by conventional physics paradigms. Throughout history, we have proven time and time again that what we previously thought impossible was just misunderstood. It was once laughable to suggest that the world could be a sphere. It was once laughable to suggest that information could travel without the need for wires. It was once laughable to suggest that we could travel by air. I believe we are again at the forefront of something truly incredible. We are tantalisingly close to some of the most important breakthroughs of our time. Surely we've learned by now that progress is born out of unconventional thinking. The people determined enough to break through the barriers of conventionality are the trailblazers we so desperately need to lead humanity to a better world for all.

Now I would like to conduct a small exercise with you that will help me illustrate the final connection I wish to make with regard to all this geometric knowledge. Take a mental step outside of this book for a moment and become conscious of your immediate environment as you're reading. Take in all your surroundings. Take in the sights, the smells, the sounds. Forget anything that's worrying or stressing you for the time being and drop any preoccupations. Observe the people around you if there are any, or the objects that surround you. Observe your mood, observe how it feels to be in your body, and observe any thoughts passing through. Now shift your perspective to the district or suburb you are in. Paint a picture in your mind of the birds-eye view of the area you are in. Look at how small everything is. Imagine all the people milling about like ants. Hear the distant symphony of sounds down below you. Watch the flow of traffic in your mind's eye if there are cars. Now slowly feel your perspective begin to zoom out of your district or suburb until you can see your whole city or township. Look at the roads and waterways and imagine they're like a network of veins and arteries. Look at the way nature organises itself. Now continue zooming out until you can see your country, then your continent, then the entire planet. Take stock of where humanity stands at this time on the earth. Now continue zooming out until the earth is like a tiny grain of sand. Keep going until you can picture Venus and Mars, then Mercury and Jupiter. Now take in the entire solar system. Watch as all of the planets orbit around the sun on their own paths. Now take in the whole Milky Way galaxy. Continue to zoom out in your mind until the Milky Way looks like something you could hold in your hand. Inside this tiny swirling galaxy are more than 100 billion planets! Now consider that there are more than 100 billion galaxies like the Milky Way that each contain more than 100 billion planets. The number of planets in 100 billion galaxies looks something like the number 1 with 22 zeroes after it! Let's pretend for a moment that there are more than 100 billion universes, each holding 100 billion galaxies, and each of those holding 100 billion planets. Is your brain in knots yet? Well... now you get a picture of the infinite nature of the cosmos... it's NEVER-ENDING! At least, that's the general consensus among quantum physicists.

Now, consider the sheer arrogance of humanity in suggesting that extra-terrestrial races are a laughable prospect. The suggestion that they are a laughable prospect

is laughable in itself! Are we that bleeding stupid as a
species that we think Earth is at the centre of the cosmos?
Do we really think humanity is the pinnacle of all that
exists? Out of the trillions upon trillions of planets out
there in the abyss of space do we think there aren't other
races who have evolved far beyond us and mastered the
ability of inter-dimensional travel? We must be the joke of
the cosmos if we're really that backwards! If you think in
terms of the scale of the great cosmic expanse we must
seem primitive to many other life-forms out there. I can
imagine them saying in their own language, 'Look at those
homo sapiens. They are still working out how to live
together without destroying themselves.' I wish I could
apologise on behalf of humanity for that but it's more
important that we act on it instead, and get ourselves out of
this terrible predicament we're in.

I hear some of you asking, 'If there are more highly
evolved races out there capable of inter-planetary and
inter-dimensional travel, how come we haven't received
any form of communication from any of them?'

The evidence strongly indicates we have. There have
been over 10,000 reported crop circles on our planet in a
great many countries over a great many decades. Of
course, some of these are human-made hoaxes and some of
them are human-made art pieces and corporate advertising
PR stunts. However, many of these crop circles simply
cannot be explained as the product of humans stomping
through crop fields in the middle of the night with boards
and string. These crop circles are completely flawless, with
no rough edges and containing dazzlingly complex and

precise geometric patterns. The man-made crop circles are crude and can easily be told apart from the others. Let's take a look at a genuine crop circle, formed in Milk Hill, England, in 2001 (Figure 5e). This particular crop formation was photographed many times from many different angles, and appeared in under 4 hours in the dead of night in the pouring rain, leaving no muddy footprints the next day. It is over 300 metres in diameter and contains 409 perfect circles.

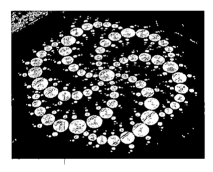

Figure 5e: The Milk Hill formation (2001).

IMAGE CREDIT: Lucy Pringle.

Hoaxers? I'd like to see humans even *attempt* to make such a perfect formation in dry conditions in broad daylight over the entire day! Scientists who study the genuine crop formations (and I say scientists because there is an official area of scientific study dedicated to documenting and researching these phenomena) have decoded these strange symbols and found that they contain a mathematical and a scientific language. Foster Gamble, new energy researcher and visionary, shows proof in his documentary, *Thrive*, that the Milk Hill fractal pattern is a 2D representation of a 3D magnetic toroidal field, or torus (Figure 5f).

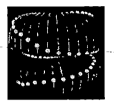

Figure 5f: A *toroidal field*.

He believes the torus to be a crucial component in understanding universal field theory, and so does Nassim Haramein, who refers to the toroidal field in many of his presentations. *Thrive* is a documentary with a great deal of vision, and I also recommend viewing it if you get the chance. When we look at more of these fascinating crop formations, we can begin to see the connections between these patterns and the geometric knowledge of ancient civilizations I have discussed throughout this chapter. Here's a 2D representation of Buckminster Fuller's 3D vector equilibrium system (Figure 5g).

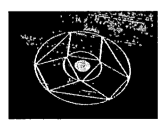

Figure 5g: A 2D representation of the *vector equilibrium* in a field.

This one appeared in Wiltshire, England in 1995. How about another formation of Nassim Haramein's 64 tetrahedron grid and then proof that the grid superimposes perfectly over the top (Figures 6a and 6b)?

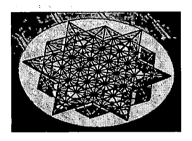

Figure 6a: Crop formation of what looks to be the *64 Tetrahedron Grid.*

Figure 6b: The *64 Tetrahedron Grid* matches up perfectly with the formation.

IMAGE CREDIT: Nassim Haramein.

Haramein also discovered that if you place a sphere perfectly around each of the tetrahedra in the 64 tetrahedron grid you are left with the flower of life pattern that has been found all over the ancient world (Figure 6c).

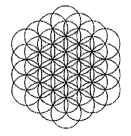

Figure 6c: Placing spheres around the *64 Tetrahedron Grid* reveals the *flower of life* pattern.

IMAGE CREDIT: Nassim Haramein.

Of course, there's a crop formation for this ancient pattern too (Figure 6d). You really can't make this stuff up!

Figure 6d: A crop formation of the *flower of life* pattern.

IMAGE CREDIT: Lucy Pringle.

Something out there in the infinite cosmos is helping us by communicating this geometric knowledge to us and letting us connect the dots. Whatever it is has very likely discovered technologies far beyond current human capabilities and is trying to pass on vital information to assist us in our evolution. Still unconvinced? How about this crop circle that appeared in Woodborough Hill, Wiltshire in 2000 (Figure 6e)?

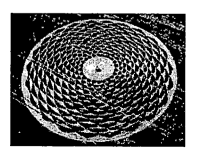

Figure 6e: 44 flawless rotations of the *Golden Mean Spiral*, 14 concentric circles and 308 standing triangles.

IMAGE CREDIT: Steve Alexander.

This highly complex formation, dubbed *The Sunflower*, features not one Golden Mean Spiral, but 44 of them in perfect rotation, as well as 14 concentric circles. A closer look at the formation reveals that these spirals are actually an illusion created by the 308 standing triangles of the formation. It's hard enough to draw a Golden Mean Spiral on paper, let alone create the *illusion* of 44 of them... in a field... in the middle of the night!

Freddy Silva, crop circle researcher, author and lecturer, explains that the crops of real formations are not damaged and show no evidence of being trampled. Instead, they are *bent* in a way that has never been replicated by humans.

He writes on his website, cropcirclesecrets.org:

In genuine formations the stems are not broken but bent, normally about an inch off the ground and near the plant's first node...

...the plants appear to be subjected to a short and intense burst of heat which softens the stems to drop just above the ground at 90 degrees, where they reharden into their new and very permanent position without damage.

Many who have spent years deciphering this mystery have encountered electro-magnetic interference on physically entering the boundary of a genuine crop circle. People have reported their compasses and GPS devices playing up, camera equipment failing and mobile phone signals disappearing completely.

In his book, *Secrets in the Fields*, Silva writes:

In recent times, a Japanese researcher found that a battery pack with fourteen hours of available power drained instantaneously the moment it touched the floor of a new crop circle. I have loaded fresh batteries into cameras and photographed successfully outside formations, yet the moment I cross a circle perimeter, the batteries are drained. Photographic cameras fare no better: reports of buckled shutters, failed drives, and loss-of-power abound. Such reports can be multiplied by the hundreds.

In 1974, Carl Sagan and Frank Drake designed a binary code radio transmission (as binary is a universal language) and sent it into the globular star cluster M13, 25,000 light years away. The coded message contained what Sagan and Drake saw as the most important information about the human species, including our numeric system, the structure of our DNA, and the atomic numbers of the primary elements for life on our planet (Figure 6f opposite). It was sent from the Arecibo radio-telescope in Puerto Rico.

In August of 2001, 27 years later, a very peculiar crop circle appeared next to the Chilbolton radio telescope in Hampshire, UK. It was a direct reply to Sagan and Drake's message (Figure 6g on p. 118).

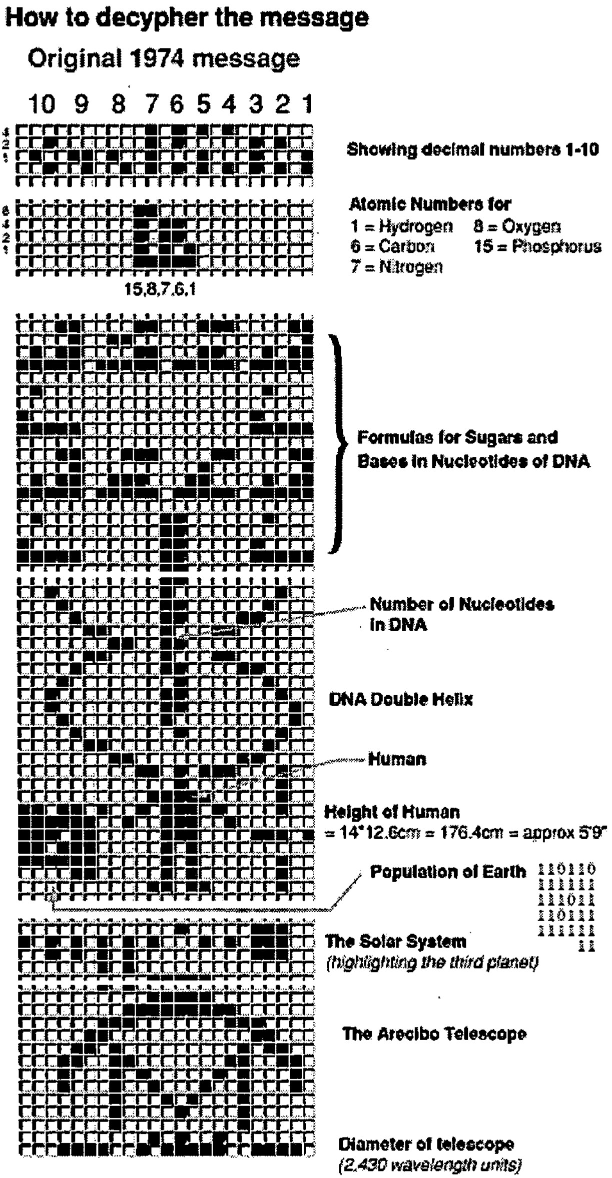

How to decypher the message

Original 1974 message

10 9 8 7 6 5 4 3 2 1

Showing decimal numbers 1-10

Atomic Numbers for
1 = Hydrogen   8 = Oxygen
6 = Carbon   15 = Phosphorus
7 = Nitrogen

15,8,7,6,1

Formulas for Sugars and Bases in Nucleotides of DNA

Number of Nucleotides in DNA

DNA Double Helix

Human

Height of Human
= 14*12.6cm = 176.4cm = approx 5'9"

Population of Earth   110110
111111
111011
110111
111111
11

The Solar System
(highlighting the third planet)

The Arecibo Telescope

Diameter of telescope
(2,430 wavelength units)

Figure 6f: Sagan and Drake's binary code message explained.

IMAGE CREDIT: Paul Vigay.

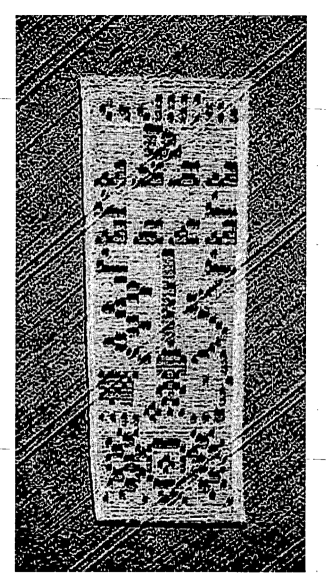

Figure 6g: A reply to the 1974 transmission next
to the Chilbolton radio telescope in Hampshire,
UK, 27 years later.

The main differences as noted by the binary code response were that the extra-terrestrial species claimed to have the additional atomic element of silicon, an extra strand of DNA, a change in the number of nucleotides, a different solar system configuration, a more complex transmission device they used to communicate with, a much shorter physical height and a much larger head in relation to their body. Paul Vigay explains these differences in greater detail at the website:

http://www.cropcircleresearch.com/articles/arecibo.html.

One year earlier, in the same month, another crop circle had been reported and photographed in exactly the same spot in the same field next to the Chilbolton radio telescope. This formation resembles the exact same transmission device as depicted at the base of the reply from 2001 (Figure 6h).

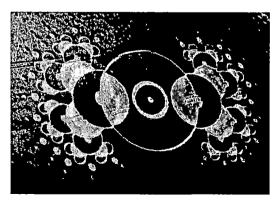

Figure 6h: A crop formation featuring the same radio transmission device depicted at the bottom of Figure 6g.

It is very important to note that the media ignored this message and no human has since claimed ownership of it. Could this extra-terrestrial species depicted in the binary code reply be the same species responsible for all the other genuine crop circles? That's for you to decide.

One thing is certain. The universe deals in these geometrical principles. Like music, it is a language all of us recognise and resonate with. When I ask people what they think about mathematics education in schools, the common consensus is that there is very little attempt to teach the *application* of mathematics principles. When I was in school, I remember learning all kinds of equations, formulas, rules and convoluted algebraic expressions. Just because I remember learning them at the time doesn't mean I still remember them. I have forgotten most of the material I learned in mathematics lessons in high school. Why? Because none of it had any meaning in my life... none whatsoever! It was just a jumble of meaningless numbers and letters, and I, like many others, had a tough time with mathematics in my later years at school. Mathematics education is a left-brain dominant area. It favours the parts rather than the whole. So what happens to all the visual learners, the dreamers, the artists, when they are forced to learn algorithms that have no bearing on their lives? They become alienated by the education system.

The truth about mathematics is that it is not just a bunch of rules and equations and pointless algebra, it is a *code* that is connected to everything in existence. It is the syntax of the universe... and it is accessible to everyone! The beauty of sacred geometry is that it appeals to both the right-brain and the left-brain. It is both artistic and organised, both contemplative and practical. There is no need for children to be alienated by mathematics. We simply need to approach it from a new angle. When children are able to connect the dots in this way, they will develop a newfound respect for the natural world around them and everything that exists in the infinite expanse of the cosmos.

We do not inherit the earth from our ancestors, we borrow it from our children.

Native American Proverb

Natural Equilibrium

Nature has given us everything we have ever needed to survive as a species, yet somewhere along the line of our evolution, we seem to have forgotten that. As a result of humanity's ignorance, we are now laying waste to a planet that gave us such abundance to begin with. If we continue to bite the hand that feeds us, our existence will face a threat of its own. We have the intelligence and the means necessary to prevent the destruction of our ecosystems and the poisoning of our atmosphere, so there is no reason why we continue to allow corrupt governments and corporations to ravage the land in the name of monetary profit. Instead of clean, renewable energy solutions, the system still relies on oil, coal, natural gas and nuclear fission power, which are causing significant damage to our environment. Why does the system rely on these out-dated forms of energy production? Because those in power have a lot of money invested in them and are only interested in the preservation of their businesses. This comes at the expense of every living organism on the planet, so it is imperative we do not sit back and let it happen. To create a better world for all, we first need to be aware of the extent to which our planet is being abused and how this affects life on earth. This is our home. It is all we have.

The Amazon rainforest in South America is being destroyed for corporate gain. A staggering 20% of the world's largest and most biodiverse rainforest has been completely razed within the last 40 years. One fifth... gone! The Amazon is home to millions of different plant, tree and animal species, but as a result of deforestation, those numbers are rapidly falling. You can actually see how such a large chunk of the Amazon has been wiped out over the years if you access Google's EarthEngine tool, which shows a time-lapse of our planet between 1984 and 2012. As you watch the time-lapse, you can see the dark green colour of South America gradually disappearing. It's a sobering picture of reality. According to Brazil's environment minister, Izabella Teixeira, 10,739 square kilometres of rainforest were razed between 2012 and 2014.

Prior to 2006, commercial soy bean farming was one of the major causes of deforestation in the Amazon basin. The soy beans were used to feed livestock for the meat industry. A moratorium was put in place between 2006 and 2014 which barred the soy industry from selling any produce linked to Amazonian deforestation. As a result, rates of deforestation decreased considerably after 2006. Due to a hard fought battle won by groups rallying for the protection of the Amazon, the moratorium has been extended to 2016. After 2016, however, if this ban is lifted, the soy industry will have free reign to start felling thousands of square kilometres of rainforest again.

In Ecuador, oil drilling in the Amazon caused wide-spread pollution and destroyed the livelihoods of the many tribal communities who called it home there. After a 17 year legal battle, ChevronTexaco was found guilty in 2011 of wastewater dumping in local rivers and streams between 1964 and 1990, and causing contamination of the water supply. The Ecuadorian court ruled that the oil giant pay $19 billion in fines and damages, but Chevron has since managed to hold up legal proceedings and send the case back to the United States where the decision was then reversed. Financial records dug up by lawyer Steven Donziger, who represented the plaintiffs against ChevronTexaco, showed that the judge ruling in favour of Chevron, Lewis Kaplan, had investments in the corporation. The case has since been regarded as one of the worst legal disasters in history and serves to highlight the shortcomings of our justice system. Despite a huge public outcry, permits have been handed out by the Ecuadorian government to oil companies that allow them to commence oil drilling in the Amazon basin from 2016. It is important that humanity stands up to this threat against its biosphere. We need our Amazon. Not only is it one of the most biodiverse regions on the planet, but it is also a major source of the world's oxygen.

Deforestation is also occurring on the island of Borneo, in large part due to industrial palm oil plantations. Palm oil is an ingredient in various cosmetics, soaps and many food products. The increased production of palm oil in the Malaysian and Indonesian rainforests over the years has caused a large percentage of those forests to disappear, along with the orangutans inhabiting them. Some of these orangutans are rescued by environmental workers, but many more are shot on sight. Making conscious consumer decisions and choosing to avoid products that contain palm oil will go a long way in thwarting these companies who show little regard for the natural world.

The destruction of mangroves worldwide is also a big problem people need to be aware of. Mangroves prevent both large-scale flooding and soil erosion, and they store more carbon dioxide than rainforests do, making the air in nearby cities breathable. Vandana Shiva, environmental activist and author, says that Mumbai's mangrove trees are being wiped out to make way for shrimp farming aquaculture. She says that industrial shrimp farmers pump sea water on to the land, causing damage to local farming plots. The livelihoods of local fishermen are also affected by the establishment of these shrimp plantations. When the 2004 tsunami ravaged South Asia, regions that had been largely cleared of their mangroves suffered much greater damage than areas where mangroves had been untouched. Instead of funding projects to preserve the mangroves, the World Bank immediately funded the rebuilding of the industrial shrimp farms. You can see a trend here, can't you? The corporatocracy and banking cartels calling the shots will do anything to protect their bottom line without any regard for environmental consequence.

Air pollution is another major issue affecting countries all over the world, and smog levels in China and India are verging on catastrophic. Air pollution in Beijing has reached a point twenty times the safe limit and is widely cited as the number one cause of death in China. Just type 'China pollution' into an image search on the internet and you'll very quickly see what I mean. While Chinese officials largely ignore the impact of coal production plant emissions on the environment, it is clear that their coal industry is the main cause of air pollution. China produces as much coal as the rest of the world *combined*, and they are showing no signs of clamping down on industrial coal emissions. Instead, they are clamping down on things like open-air barbecues and fireworks for Chinese New Year. I'm not actually kidding. The Chinese government introduced measures to prohibit the use of barbecues and is considering banning fireworks during Spring Festival. Rather than a decrease in China's coal production in the last year, there has been an *increase*. It's complete madness. The air purifier mask industry has boomed, so much so that masks are now coming in custom designs and treated as fashion accessories. I know I've singled out China but the reality is that air pollution is increasingly becoming a serious global environmental problem, and the only way to combat it is through clean energy solutions. I'll come back to this point a bit further on.

The Fukushima disaster that forced the evacuation of more than 150,000 people from their homes in Japan serves as a sobering reminder of the serious dangers of nuclear power. In 2011, a magnitude 9.0 earthquake caused a tsunami to hit the Fukushima Daiichi nuclear power plant, triggering a series of meltdowns and releasing enormous amounts of radiation into the atmosphere. Katsutaka Idogawa, former mayor of Futaba, resigned from his political position to become an advocate against nuclear power. Prior to the Fukushima disaster, he was a supporter of nuclear energy, but now after seeing the effects of the radiation poisoning, he is trying to tell the world to stop using nuclear power. Idogawa says that the government is telling people they can safely move back home even though radiation levels in the Fukushima Prefecture are still dangerously high:

The Fukushima Prefecture has launched the 'Come Home' campaign. In many cases, evacuees are forced to return... the air contamination decreased a little, but the soil contamination remains the same... and there are still about 2 million people living in the prefecture who have all sorts of medical issues. Authorities claim this has nothing to do with the fallout. I demanded that the authorities substantiate their claim in writing but they ignored my request. There are some terrible things going on in Fukushima... I talked to local authorities in different places in Fukushima, but no one would listen to me. They believe what the government says, when in reality the radiation is still there. This is killing children. They die of heart conditions, asthma, leukaemia, thyroiditis... but authorities still hide the truth from us, and I don't know why.

- Katsutaka Idogawa

Farmers working in the Fukushima Prefecture are being forced to sell produce that show clear signs of contamination, and are having to live with the guilt of knowing they are selling food they would not eat themselves. In a public hearing in June of 2013 between prefecture citizens and the government, farmers expressed their outrage at the Japanese authorities for allowing contaminated food to be sold on to consumers. The following is a statement from one such farmer:

The consumers assume there is no radiation in the food they buy... we farmers know better. We feel guilty about growing it and selling it. We won't eat it ourselves, but we sell it.

Even though the farmers had measured abnormally high caesium levels in their soil, the government responded by denying the farmers' claims and referring to them as 'rumours'. Rates of suicide among farmers in the Prefecture have increased dramatically after the Fukushima incident.

The Tokyo Electric Power Company (TEPCO) has been criticised heavily for its complicity in the corruption surrounding Fukushima, and for their refusal to disclose the truth about the radiation situation. TEPCO has been storing radioactive water in tanks, which are continually growing in number. These tanks have now started leaking. On top of this, TEPCO has started dumping Fukushima reactor groundwater into the Pacific Ocean.

Former Prime Minister, Naoto Kan, who resigned due to the political pressure surrounding his handling of the Fukushima crisis, has now become a vocal critic of nuclear power. His successor, Shinzo Abe, has no intention of cutting the use of nuclear power. In fact, the current Japanese government is trying to start up another nuclear plant in Sendai.

You'd think the Chernobyl disaster in Ukraine (formerly USSR) was enough of a wake-up call for humanity to phase out nuclear power. The death toll from radiation poisoning caused by the Chernobyl nuclear reactor explosion in 1986 is estimated at around 1 million at the moment. Even after the Fukushima meltdown put the entire future of Japan at risk, their government still insists on restarting nuclear power. We cannot afford another nuclear crisis. There are hundreds of nuclear power plants still in operation around the world. That's hundreds of ticking time bombs. People, and especially the youth of today, need to be aware of this. It cannot continue. Enough madness already.

In 2010, a British Petroleum (BP) oil rig exploded in the Gulf of Mexico, killing 11 of their workers and spilling 200 million gallons of oil into the sea. Even now, five years on, the effects of the spill are still being felt by the ocean wildlife in the gulf. The National Wildlife Federation (NWF) reported that 14 different species of animals are still showing symptoms of oil exposure, including dolphins, turtles and sperm whales. The explosion was found to be a result of gross technical negligence on the part of the oil giant. BP has managed to delay court proceedings until this year (2015). Damages are currently projected at around $17 billion. The BP oil spill in the Gulf of Mexico is regarded as one of the worst environmental disasters in history, and the oil company is still evading accountability.

In 1989, a similar disaster occurred at Prince William Sound in Alaska, when the Exxon Valdez oil tanker struck Bligh Reef, spilling more than 11 million gallons of crude oil into the waters. The oil washed up on beaches up to 650 miles away, devastating the marine wildlife, and killing more than 250,000 sea birds. ExxonMobil, formerly Exxon, is still battling the court system 25 years after the event, in the longest-running environmental court case in history. According to GoogleEarth's archive database, there have been hundreds of significant oil spills recorded all around the world.

Now all of the 'Big Oil' players are flocking to the many regions of the Arctic to commence drilling. Like we haven't left enough of a trail of destruction on this planet, we have to pollute the ice-water too? Humanity is still in the early stages of research with regard to the Arctic ecosystems and environment. We do not yet have the technology to clean up oil spills on ice, and the climate in Arctic regions is such that an oil spill is inevitable.

These oil juggernauts have free reign to do what they want without public consent, all the money in the world to buy legal immunity, and a complete disregard for the natural equilibrium. We must change the trajectory we are on if we are to progress as a species. The good news is that the oil companies do not have all the power... we do. If the world embraced new energy technologies, the multi-trillion dollar fossil fuel empires would collapse like a house of cards. We cannot rely on our governments and politicians to take radical action. It simply will not happen that way because they continue to back fossil fuels. Our governments do not serve the people. They serve their own selfish interests. It is up to us to realise the power we have and to lead the way with new energy technologies. We have to trailblaze the way forward ourselves, no matter what the cost. Our evolution depends on it.

Solar power has incredible potential as a renewable energy solution. The sun provides us with an unlimited supply of energy, which when converted, does not release harmful pollutants into the atmosphere. We have enough space in all the major deserts to power the world many, many times over. The technology for solar conversion is very quickly becoming cheaper and more efficient than ever, with 'peel-and-stick' panels and concentrated solar power (CSP) replacing the clunky silicon panels of old. Concentrated solar power works kind of like the ancient Archimedean death ray, in that it focuses solar energy in on one point, by reflecting the rays of the sun.

When considering the potential pitfalls of desert-based solar plants, the first thing that came to my mind was cleaning and panel maintenance. Given their location, the panels would be subjected to considerable amounts of dust build-up on a regular basis. Then I thought, 'What if we had little panel-cleaning robots that could work diligently and automatically?' Then I found out that such robots already exist and are in use in desert power-plants already. The robots even scavenge their own power from the sun with their own in-built solar panels. Genius!

There really is no reason why a much larger percentage of the world's energy doesn't come from solar. These ridiculously conservative targets from our politicians for renewable energy usage are an insult to our intelligence and an insult to the crisis this planet faces. The UK aims for 15% renewable energy by 2020. According to the International Energy Agency, the global energy target for solar is 27% by 2050. Australia, a desert-rich land that should be leading the charge in this area, is actually going backwards, having recently cut its renewable energy support considerably. Way to go, Tony Abbott. We can't afford to take another hundred years to phase out fossil fuels and nuclear power completely. Not to mention we'll be out of oil and gas completely in another 50-60 years the way it's going. Germany gets around 30% of its energy from renewable sources at the moment, and Denmark gets more than 40%. The rest of the world needs to wake up fast and follow suit.

Wind power accounts for only 4% of the world's total energy output, yet it is much cheaper to run than fossil fuel industries and it is completely clean. Denmark is leading the way in the wind energy sector, with 34% of their total energy output coming from wind power. Much of that percentage comes from wind farms built offshore, as there is greater wind potential offshore. Offshore wind farms also ensure that land is not being deforested to make way for the turbines. Denmark is aiming for 50% wind power by 2020. Take that, David Cameron, and your pitiful 15% renewables target for 2020! China is pushing for an expansion in wind power, but it's still a very long way off taking over its coal output. Theoretically, we could easily power the entire planet on solar and wind alone. The trillion-dollar energy monopolies do not want that, however, and are doing everything in their power to preserve their empires.

Renewable energy solutions are not just limited to solar and wind. These two sources are just the tip of the iceberg. Geothermal power is another viable alternative that taps into the natural heat below the earth's surface. Geothermal energy is abundant, clean and cost-effective. So why is it barely being utilised? There has been so much talk surrounding solar and wind that geothermal has been largely ignored. Though some countries have greater access to geothermal energy than others due to their tectonic activity, geothermal has enormous potential for the world. 30% of Iceland's electricity supply comes from geothermal sources. The US technically has the largest geothermal industry in the world, but it only accounts for a measly 0.3% of their national energy production. Indonesia, which relies mostly on coal and oil, is letting so much potential go to waste. They are sitting on around 40% of the world's full geothermal potential.

Wave power is yet another source of clean, renewable energy that we should be harnessing. Almost no one has heard of it, but the idea of utilising the Herculean power of nature's oceans is really quite clever. A handful of small wave power companies are already in operation. Pelamis, a Scotland-based wave energy company, leads the charge. They have succeeded through rigorous testing programs and are now working on commercial-scale projects. Wave power is actually more reliable than solar and wind power, as waves occur consistently around the clock. Wave farms also require considerably less space than wind farms do. With the length of coastline that countries like Australia have, we'd be crazy not to utilise as much of that potential as possible.

Tidal power, which is different from wave power, uses underwater turbines to convert the energy from the tidal flow into electricity. The tides are more predictable than the sun and the wind, which puts tidal power on par with wave power in terms of reliability. South Korea is investing a great deal of money in tidal power, with two major projects in the works already. One of those projects is set to be the world's largest tidal farm.

Then there's nuclear 'hot fusion' technology, which produces small amounts of radiation compared to nuclear fission. As mentioned in one of the previous chapters, Doug Coulter is working on an open-source model for nuclear fusion in his back-woods cabin, with no bureaucratic red tape to hold him back. He is currently working on remote-controlling the entire process from afar, so he can safely achieve fusion without being affected by the radiation. He has a channel on YouTube where he uploads regular videos of his progress. I encourage you to get behind Doug and his work. He is closer to achieving full-blown nuclear hot fusion than any of the top-tier scientists at Lockheed Martin who are receiving billions of dollars in funding. Of course, they won't like to admit that.

Nuclear 'hot fusion' is amazing, but it's nothing compared to 'cold fusion'. Cold fusion is more or less the holy grail of nuclear physics. In theory, the process of cold fusion would produce incredible amounts of energy, so much so that the entire planet could easily run on cold fusion technology alone, including the transport industry. The only resource required to generate cold fusion is heavy water (deuterium oxide), which is a thousand times cheaper than oil. It would also produce zero radiation, unlike other forms of nuclear energy. In 1989, Stanley Pons and Martin Fleischmann, two chemists from the University of Utah, claimed they had discovered fusion taking place at room temperature. On presenting their findings to the mainstream scientific community, Pons & Fleischmann were lambasted, ridiculed and scoffed at. The most virulent criticism came from members in the 'hot fusion' sector of MIT, who slammed Pons & Fleischmann in a damning report refuting their claims. Eugene Mallove, who was chief science writer at the MIT news office at the time, said that the individuals who created this report against Pons & Fleischmann altered the data dramatically to suit their position:

That data is scientific fraud as far as I'm concerned and many other people are concerned. It was represented as a negative result when it was positive.

- Eugene Mallove

Mallove, who completed a Master of Science degree in Aeronautical and Astronautical Engineering from MIT and a Doctorate in Environmental Health Sciences from Harvard, asked for a review of the data from MIT officials, and was denied the request. At the time, cold fusion was receiving a thrashing in the media due to MIT's firm stance. Mallove resigned from his position in protest and started up his own freelance publication, *Infinite Energy* magazine, which published up-to-date findings and breakthroughs by the cold fusion community. He also established the New Energy Research Laboratory. Mallove then wrote the documentary, *Cold Fusion: Fire from Water*, which tells of the extensive developments in this field that are being largely ignored by conventional scientists and academics. If you want to know the truth about cold fusion, watch this documentary. Mallove was determined to champion the cold fusion movement, despite being derided as a 'fringe scientist', and *Infinite Energy* magazine ended up going out to 38 countries. He knew the impact cold fusion would have on the trillion-dollar energy empires:

I think that the electric power grid will absolutely wither away. I think automobiles, trucks, trains, planes, all forms of transportation, will use this new powerful energy source. The writing is on the wall. The fossil fuel age is about to end.

Mallove also claimed to have uncovered corruption within the US Patent Office surrounding patents for cold fusion.

In an interview[4], he stated:

---

[4] See *References* for source of this interview

There has been an extraordinary abrogation of basic legal responsibility at the Patent Office for example, and at the Department of Energy, on the matter of cold fusion... there is serious criminal activity going on that ultimately must be rooted out if the cold fusion new energy revolution is to go forward.

In 2004, Eugene Mallove was found bludgeoned to death in the yard of his childhood home in Norwich.

In the 1980s, Stanley Meyer invented a working water fuel cell that could run any car using regular tap water. He had it independently tested, received patents from the US, Europe and Japan, and was approached by multiple investors, including officials from the US Department of Defense. There was no doubt that the technology worked. Meyer was offered a very large sum of money by an Arabian oil company to sign over his patents and rights for the invention, which he refused. In 1998, Stanley and his twin-brother, Steven Meyer, met two Belgian investors at a Cracker Barrel diner. After a toast with cranberry juice, Stan abruptly stood up, ran outside and began vomiting violently. His brother ran outside after him and watched him die. Stan's last words to his brother were, 'I've been poisoned.' This account has been verified by Meyer's own family. See *References*.

An Australian inventor, Les Banki, tells of what happened to his close colleague and fellow inventor:

One of our colleagues, who had been running his car on water, reckons it is twenty six times more powerful than petrol... and he used it for several years... somehow, the news got out and one day he got visitors, and he was told to dump the engine or else. Three weeks later, the man was dead... and the coroner's finding was that he fell off the back of a train; he was drunk. Now, it happened that he didn't drink.

Daniel Dingel, a Filipino inventor, had been working on his water fuel cell for over 30 years. Many people, who expressed interest from all corners of the globe, came to Manila to test Dingel's Toyota Corolla, which ran on ordinary salt water from the ocean. On verifying that the car was not connected to the gas at all, those who witnessed it running on water withdrew their skepticism. Dingel's goal was for his invention to help solve the problem of pollution and to help humanity. With any money he was to make from the invention, he wanted to set up a foundation to give that money directly to the Filipino people. He ended up spending many years fighting to get his technology on the market. At the age of 83, Dingel was charged with 'estafa' (swindling) and sentenced to 20 years in prison, where he died a year later.

In the mid-1990s, a self-taught backyard mechanic from New South Wales in Australia, known only as Joe, created a very unique water fuel cell that appeared to tap the energy from the zero-point energy field; what Tesla called 'the aether'. After proving the legitimacy of his strange invention to friends and impartial onlookers alike, the device became known as the 'Joe Cell'. Its inventor, Joe, doesn't even know *why* it works, only that it *does* work. He drove all the way from his home in Northern New South Wales to Melbourne, Victoria, and back again, on the Joe

Cell. Word got out, one thing led to another, and before he knew it, the Federal Government was trying to buy him out. Noah Yamore, who was a close friend and confidant, said the government offered Joe $10,000 and a new car if he signed over all the rights to the fuel cell. Not surprisingly, he rejected the offer. Soon after, the Australian Secret Intelligence Service (ASIS) told Joe it was not in his best interests to continue his line of research. Joe ignored ASIS' threat.

At the time, he had been freely giving Joe Cells away to people. He had no interest in making money off them. Joe claims government people had been following him everywhere, bugging him and threatening him. *Beyond 2000*, an Australian television series reporting on groundbreaking inventions at the time, asked Joe to be interviewed for the show. Before agreeing to the interview, he received a threatening phone call telling him that there would be dire consequences for his family if he went ahead with the filming. At that point, Joe pulled the plug on the show. He has now abandoned his work on the Joe Cell and does not want to be contacted.

Bill Williams, a US inventor, managed to replicate the Joe Cell and run his truck off it. He gave this account of what happened to him while driving home in his gas-free truck one day:

I stopped to check the post connection point on the cell. I was standing in front of my truck, and this late model 2005 or 2006 Ford Explorer pulled up and parked diagonally in front of my truck. The driver got out of the rig and approached me. At about the same time, the passenger opened his door. The driver stated that he wanted me to stop working on all forms of alternative energy. He also stated that he knew everything about me, my family, and all my projects past and present. At about that time the passenger held up a file that was about 2 or so inches thick. He opened it up and showed me telephone transcripts, emails, messages from the groups that I had belonged to. They knew where my kids worked, the times they are at work, also my wife's working hours, my grandkids' school etc. They knew everything. The driver said that if I did not stop working on this that there would be other consequences. He also stated that he wanted me to post that I was no longer working in this field and to destroy all my work.

Williams complied with the threat, destroyed his work, and has not pursued research into the Joe Cell since.

These same scenarios have played out time and time again in the new energy field. I mentioned Nikola Tesla and the suppression of his Wardenclyffe Tower project in the previous chapter. Thomas Henry Moray invented a device in the 1920s called the *Moray Radiant Energy Device*, which converted zero-point energy into electricity. Moray's applications to the US Patent Office were rejected. He received threats on a regular basis and barely survived a shotgun assault in his lab in 1940.

Adam Trombly, another proponent of zero-point energy technologies, has been issued gag orders, survived several assassination attempts on his life, and has had all of his work confiscated:

Every single technology that I have either invented or co-produced is no longer in my possession... I've had a number of attempts on my life through really serious poisonings. My wife has had to revive me and give me CPR.

                              - Adam Trombly

Inventors like Bruce DePalma, John Hutchison, John Bedini and Gary Vesperman have all experienced the suppression of their work in the new energy field. Vesperman compiled a list of 95 new energy suppression incidents in a document titled *Energy Invention Suppression Cases*. A web address for this document can be found in the *References* section of this book.

Though it can be difficult for many to stomach the degree to which these inventions are being kept from the public domain, it's not all that surprising when you take into account what is at stake for the suppressors. If any of these inventions were mass-produced, it would be the death of the most powerful industry in the world - the energy industry.

It's goodbye ExxonMobil, goodbye oil, goodbye coal, goodbye linear transmission of electricity through power lines... all that gone... unfortunately, it's someone's 200 trillion dollar piggy bank. This information coming out would completely change geopolitical power more than anything in recorded human history.

       - Steven Greer, M.D. (Director of *The Disclosure Project*)

The energy industry would rather see humanity's growth stunted than allow for its own obsolescence. Our entire species is being threatened by the withholding of this technology, so it now becomes vital for us to educate as many people as possible about this abuse of human rights. School children should be shown demonstrations of new energy devices and analysing them in science labs. Kids need to see that this technology exists. They're being kept in the dark. All of us are.

The vast majority of people don't seem to pay much attention to a problem unless that problem arrives on their doorstep. Well, this information affects every single person on the planet. If this technology got out, every human being would have access to clean, endless, free energy, for the rest of their lives. The knowledge that such a future is being intentionally prevented should make all of our blood boil.

The first step to combating this problem is to spread awareness. Tell people about it! Get the information out there. If enough people know about it, then these inventions will be popping up at a rate that the energy cartels will be unable to suppress. If you're an inventor in the new energy field, open-source your work to the world. Give the plans to everybody. Demonstrate your inventions to schools, universities and other public forums. Make a name for yourself. Don't give the oil companies a chance to sweep it under the rug. They can handle a rogue inventor here and there, but they can't handle a zero-point energy *movement*. If inventors become known in the public sphere, then any attempts at suppression will just serve to wake even more people up to what's going on. Sooner or later, the house of cards will fall. It's so important that these technologies see the light of day.

Respecting our natural world is not just about preventing environmental damage and embracing clean energy technologies. I do not believe we can achieve natural equilibrium without first attempting to better understand nature itself. The root of the problem lies in our disconnect with mother Earth. Plants have been used as medicines for many thousands of years. Indigenous shamanism has been around almost as long as humans have, and is still practised widely among native cultures. In the introduction of this book, I spoke of the profound healing properties of the ayahuasca vine. Ayahuasca, a liquid extract produced by South American shamans, has been shown to be effective in the treatment of various addictions and mental illnesses. So effective, in fact, that an entire tourism industry has spawned in Peru because of it. There are now hundreds of retreats where people go to participate in formal ayahuasca ceremonies. Though I encourage people with an interest in the healing benefits of this plant to take part in a Peruvian ayahuasca ceremony (as I will likely at some point), I must warn people that there are also unethical individuals posing as reputable ayahuasca shamans. Accounts have emerged of these imposters molesting and physically assaulting tourists during ayahuasca ceremonies. I don't want this to deter people from going to Peru to try ayahuasca, but do your research first. This is not something you should rush into.

Go through the proper channels and make sure that you are going to a reputable ayahuasca retreat.

The iboga plant is a West-African rainforest shrub with remarkable healing properties as well. Ibogaine is a natural substance produced by the iboga plant that is useful in the treatment of opiate addiction. Case studies have shown that ibogaine can significantly reduce dependency on heroin and methadone. Like ayahuasca, ibogaine takes the patient on a lengthy visual journey through their subconscious that forces them to confront the true nature of their behaviour. Both ayahuasca and ibogaine are illegal in most countries in the world, including the US.

What if I told you that there was already a known cure for cancer, and that this cure was being suppressed? Would you believe me if I told you that this cure was actually cannabis? To be clear, I'm not talking about smoking it. Though cannabis in its smokable form has medicinal benefits as well, I'm referring to a thick liquid substance produced by the plant, known as *cannabis oil*. This medicine is a game-changer, and we are being kept completely in the dark about it.

Rick Simpson has been producing cannabis hemp oil from his backyard in Nova Scotia, Canada, since 2003. He gives it away on a donation basis to people who have serious illnesses like cancer. He has never intended to make a profit from it. He only wants to spread awareness about the medicine, and for people to experience its healing power for themselves. In 1997, Rick suffered a serious head injury for which he was hospitalised. The pharmaceutical drugs he was given to treat his condition did not help, and his doctors gave up on him. Having heard about hemp oil, he decided to produce it himself and take it as a medicine. His condition gradually improved and he was soon fighting fit again. In 2003, after his doctor had found several skin cancers on his body, Rick turned again to hemp oil. He put the oil on two bandages and applied them to the areas of skin cancer. In four days, the cancers were gone. Since that time, Rick has wanted to share the cure with as many people as possible.

One such person was Jim LeBlanc, who visited Rick in 2007 in a last-ditch effort to beat terminal stomach cancer. He had tried chemotherapy and radiation therapy which had done more harm than good. Here is what Jim had to say about his decision to visit Rick's garden:

I didn't really want to come down here, but my better half forced me to come, and I did ... and that's the best move that I ever made in my life. That's when things changed, you know. I started eating, I started feeling better ... I walked out of here with hope, which I didn't have when I first came in.

Jim was at death's door and kicked his terminal cancer by taking hemp oil.

Tommy Chong, of *Cheech & Chong* fame, found out about cannabis oil as a medicine for cancer treatment after watching Rick Simpson's documentary, *Run From the Cure* (2008). Chong had prostate cancer which he has now overcome with the help of cannabis oil.

It is a medicine. It's effective medicine. It works, I've seen it.
— Tommy Chong

UK father Mike Wilson decided to go down the cannabis oil route for his 5 year old son, Jayden, who had a Grade-4 brain tumour. In September of 2014, After having tried everything to save their son's life, including conventional radiotherapy, Mike and his wife figured they had to give cannabis oil treatment a go. Even though it was illegal to obtain in the UK without proper medical consent, Jayden's parents were lucky enough to have a doctor prescribe the oil legally. Three months down the road, Jayden is now taking nothing but natural cannabis oil, and is making a gradual recovery.

A mother in Minnesota is facing two years in prison and a $6000 fine for treating her 15 year old son's seizures with cannabis oil. Angela Brown's son, Trey, suffered a brain injury while playing baseball, and has had to deal with violent seizures and suicidal thoughts ever since his injury. After the conventional medical establishment let her down, Angela travelled to Colorado to obtain the oil, which she says worked wonders for Trey's condition. She saw the pain disappear and for a time Trey was no longer a shell of himself. That is, until Trey's school found out about Angela's cannabis oil, and dobbed her in to the police. Authorities arrested her and confiscated the medicine. Even though marijuana is being legalised in Minnesota now, the law does not come into effect until mid-2015. The Brown family are appealing to the public to raise funds for Angela's legal defence.

During my research on cannabis oil, I was fortunate
enough to interview someone about their own success with
the medicine. For legal reasons, he asked me to refer only
to his first name, Rudolf. When I spoke to Rudolf, who is
currently living in Norway, he told me he was riddled with
health problems until hemp oil came along. In 2013, Rudolf
got food poisoning while working on an industrial oil rig
in Denmark. Soon after, he developed kidney pains and
gall bladder pains. After doctors told him it was nothing,
his condition worsened. In the following months, he
developed muscle loss, severe fatigue, skeletal pains and
numbness in his limbs. He was then diagnosed with auto-
immune disease. After doctors were unable to help Rudolf,
he managed to order some hemp oil from a state in the US
where it was legal. He said that his very first 8.33mg dose
relieved most of the pain immediately and the effects
lasted for 24 hours. While on a regular treatment of the oil,
all his symptoms started disappearing. After three days,
the crunching sound in his neck was gone. The numbness
was gone within a week, and his joint pains vanished
completely after a month. He was able to walk properly,
train in the gym and rebuild his muscle. Now he only takes
one dose of hemp oil every week or two and he's right as
rain.

I could go on with countless other miraculous accounts
of people who have treated cancer and other illnesses with
cannabis oil, but you'll find them easily enough if you look
for them. A good source of information and success stories
is: www.cureyourowncancer.org.

Why is this cure for cancer illegal in most countries in the world? Why is it being kept from the sick and dying? Chemotherapy and radiation therapy have extremely low success rates, and in most cases are a death sentence in themselves.

Rick Schiff, a San Francisco police sergeant, spoke at a Congressional Subcommittee Hearing in 1996 about how chemo and radiotherapy killed his 4 year old daughter:

It burnt her skull so bad she had second degree burns and her hair never came back. To change her diapers, we had to wear rubber gloves because her urine was so toxic. We were told, 'Sorry, we've done everything we can. Now she's going to die... probably within a couple of months.'

- Sergeant Rick Schiff, S.F.P.D.

Schiff said his daughter died due to the radiation poisoning. The cancer industry and the pharmaceutical industry both know full-well that cannabis oil can cure cancer. If you follow the money, it becomes clear why they do not want the public to find out about this medicine. Both are multi-billion dollar industries who make their money from sick people. There is no money in healthy people, and there is no money in dead people. The only money is in sick people. Along comes a cure that cannot be patented by the pharmaceutical industry and cannot be monetised by the cancer industry. That is a direct threat to their existence. These sick and twisted industries that claim they operate in the public's best interests don't care about people getting better. Once you see that their survival depends on keeping people in a state of sickness instead of health, you begin to see how backwards the *system* really is, and how detrimental it is to real human prosperity. Take any industry and the same backwards mentality almost always applies. The cosmetics and fashion industries cannot survive without keeping people in a state of insecurity. The energy industry cannot survive without people paying for something they could have for free. The media industry cannot survive without keeping people in a state of fear. The monetary system cannot survive without perpetual consumerism.

My point being, the system has failed us as a species. If you have a loved one who is suffering from cancer, or know anyone who is, tell them to try cannabis oil. There is not one shred of evidence anywhere to suggest cannabis oil has any detrimental effects to health. You have nothing to lose and everything to gain. Of course, like all plant medicines, do your research first. Not all companies claiming to sell the oil have an effective product. If in doubt, and you have access to the plant, it is easy enough to extract yourself. Though I am strongly in favour of legalization of cannabis for medical reasons, I am not to be held responsible for any breaches of the law on the basis of this information. You are accountable for your own actions should you choose to act outside of the legal system.

It is not the fault of our doctors and physicians for ignoring plant medicines like cannabis oil. Medical school trains them to endorse the use of synthetic compounds and unnatural chemicals, while disregarding the medicines nature provided us with. If doctors were to step outside the confines of their 'code of practice', they would risk losing their medical license and their reputation. They are trained to follow protocol. Therein lies the problem. Very few doctors question the medicine they are prescribing. Very few consider alternatives to pharmaceutical drugs. They are told, more or less, that there's 'a pill for every ill', and led to believe that natural medicines are asinine. I would go as far as to say that this subservience of doctors and physicians to the system begins in childhood. At school, they excel through all the tests, all the exams and all the textbooks. They are the cream of the crop. They are the students who ticked every box, fulfilled every criteria, and were obedient every step of the way. In this sense, the highest scoring students become the ideal lapdogs for the system; intelligent enough to do brain surgery, but lacking the foresight to see the forest for the trees. This is why I come back to the importance of critical thinking being taught from an early age. If kids are capable of seeing the bigger picture during their schooling years, then we won't have this poisonous trickle-down effect into all facets of society. Critical thinking is essential for human evolution. Without the ability to question old patterns, old paradigms and old behaviours, we will not be able to solve the environmental crisis this planet faces. Unless we attempt to better understand nature, respect nature and *connect* with nature, we will condemn all life on earth to the trash heap. The education system simply must adapt to the situation we are living in. Sustainability education receives very little focus in schools at present, and this needs to change as soon as possible if we are to progress as a species. Our children must be aware of these obstacles we are up against, and be given the tools necessary to come up with their own solutions to these global problems. We are at a crossroads. We can continue on our current trajectory and turn a blind eye to natural injustice, or we can take charge of our own power and restore the environment to equilibrium. The choice is ours.

We are here to awaken from the illusion of our separateness.

Thich Nhat Hanh

We Are All One

E ver since I was a small child, I couldn't understand why countries were so separate from one another. It seemed silly to me that we all had our own flags and our own national anthems. It seemed even sillier to me that our species would feel the need to assert dominance over other countries in every way imaginable. All my life, I never had one ounce of patriotism or nationalistic pride. I never felt comfortable with pledging allegiance to the Australian flag, and I never felt comfortable conforming to what society expected of me as an Australian. Being an Australian doesn't mean much to me. I haven't really felt the need to bring up my national background throughout this book until now... because it doesn't mean anything to me. I am not defined by my body, my postcode, my state, my flag, my culture or my country. The only thing that defines me is consciousness itself and everything in it. For we are not our name, we are not our skin colour, and we are not our religion. There is no 'us' and 'them'. There are no foreigners. There are no outsiders. There are no targets, no threats and no enemies. There is only consciousness; a consciousness that connects all living things in the cosmos. What I have come to realise is that we have been brought up on fear. Fear of everything. Fear of failure. Fear of debt. Fear of what other people think. Fear of terrorism. Fear of our parents. Fear of being wrong. Fear of being alone. Fear of speaking out. Fear of death. Fear of being powerless. Fear of the unknown...

Most fears are an illusion. They are false constructs put in place to keep us subservient to this system. They keep us divided in every way. They give our governments an excuse to strip us of our freedoms.

When I decided to do something about the education system, I did not want to let fear be a controlling factor in my life any longer. So I abandoned all unnecessary fear. I took a leap of faith and ventured off the beaten path. It wasn't easy. Nothing worthwhile in life ever is. I had to risk losing old friendships, leaving my job, leaving university, facing ridicule and disappointing all of my family members. It was tough to maintain the relationships that meant the most to me. It was a battle to get my parents to understand why I would do what I was doing. I didn't take a risk out of fear. I took it out of love; love for the whole human family.

I remember when I first went to Nepal and stayed with a Nepalese family in a small community in Kathmandu, one of the first things that struck me was that I kept being called 'brother' by the Nepalese people I befriended. I didn't understand at the time why they called me that, but I do now. It is because they genuinely thought of me as their own brother. They loved me like a brother. See, we are all brothers and sisters on this planet. We are not strangers. It's time to tear down the boundaries that we erect for ourselves. It's time to make the shift away from fear and into love. The suffering in this world has to end. It has gone on far too long. Your pain is my pain. Your tears are my tears. *We are all one...*

What is consciousness? John Hagelin, quantum physics researcher and Professor of Physics at the Maharishi University of Management in the US, says it is not created by the brain, and that it is instead at the very core of the universe. As John explains it so eloquently, I've provided an abridged transcript of his interview with the director of the film, *What the Bleep Do We Know* (2004), on the subject of consciousness and super string unified field theory:

With the discovery of the unified field (the so-called super string field), we now understand life is fundamentally one. At the basis of all life's diversity there is unity... and that unity, at the basis of mind and matter, is consciousness; universal consciousness...

...consciousness isn't created by the brain. It's not purely an outcome of molecular chemical processes in the brain, but is fundamental in nature; it's at the very core of nature...

...progress, in our understanding of the universe through physics over the past quarter century, has been exploring deeper levels of natural law from the macroscopic to the microscopic; from the molecular to the atomic to the nuclear to sub-nuclear levels of nature's functioning... and what we've discovered at the

core basis of the universe is a single universal field of intelligence...

...all the forces of nature, and all the so-called particles of nature (quarks, leptons, protons, neutrons) are now understood to be one. They're all just different ripples on a single ocean of existence...

...planets, trees, people, animals, we're all just waves of vibration of this underlying unified super string field...

...everyone who has grown up in the scientific world is used to the concept that we're living in a material universe; an inert universe; a universe of dead matter... and because of that, it's difficult instinctively to grasp that we're not really living in a dead universe and that the universe is overwhelmingly conscious at its basis...

...in the realm of quantum mechanics, the idea of particle is replaced by the idea of wave function... the deeper you go in the structure of natural law (the less material, the less inert, the less dead the universe is), the more alive, the more conscious the universe becomes...

...the unified field is pure abstract potential, pure abstract being, pure abstract self-aware consciousness which rises in waves of vibration to give rise to the particles, the people, everything we see in the vast universe.

In 1966, Cleve Backster, a former CIA polygraph specialist, made a startling discovery when he hooked up a polygraph machine to a common house plant. As the polygraph machine was able to measure the physiological responses of humans, Backster was curious to see how plants would react to different stimuli. After establishing a baseline reading, he first decided to dip one of the leaves into a mug of hot coffee. The polygraph reading did not change. Backster then wondered what would happen if he held a lit match to the leaf. Immediately on the thought entering his mind, the polygraph machine registered a large spike in physiological activity. Before Backster had even moved a muscle in the direction of his matches, the plant seemed to be fully aware of his intention to cause it harm. Fascinated, he wanted to see if the same reading would register if he merely pretended to burn the leaf. Astonishingly, the plant did not react at all. Only when Backster fully intended to burn the plant did the plant react.

In another experiment, Backster wanted to see if a plant would react to the death of living organisms in a separate room, without the plant having foreknowledge of their inevitable demise. He hypothesised:

There exists an as yet undefined primary perception in plant life, that animal life termination can serve as a remotely located stimulus to demonstrate this perception capability, and that this perception facility in plants can be shown to function independently of human involvement.

Backster poured brine shrimp into a small dish suspended over a pot of boiling water. The device was automated to tip the brine shrimp into the boiling water after a period of time. Backster randomised the timer so that he would have no idea when the shrimp would be sent to their doom. In another room of the lab, well out of sight of the device, he hooked up a plant to a polygraph machine. In order to ensure his own thoughts and intentions would not affect the results, Backster drove miles away from the lab until the experiment was concluded. When he returned and inspected the polygraph reading, it indicated a sharp spike in activity at the precise moment that the shrimp tipped into the pot of boiling water. The experiment was subjected to repetition and the results were found to be consistent.

Unfortunately, Backster's ground-breaking discoveries have been ridiculed by the mainstream scientific community and many scientists have refused to replicate his studies. It remains an underground area of scientific research. To see more about plant consciousness, including Backster's work from the 1960s, watch a documentary called *The Secret Life of Plants* (1979).

The late Dr. Masaru Emoto dedicated much of his life to studying the consciousness of water. In one of his experiments, Emoto subjected samples of the same water source to different types of music. He then froze each of the samples and examined the water crystals that formed as a result. These are the water samples that were exposed to Beethoven's *Pastorale*, John Lennon's *Imagine*, and heavy metal music, respectively:

Beethoven's *Pastorale*   John Lennon's *Imagine*   Heavy metal music

Emoto took his research even further and hypothesised
that words and intention would affect the formation of the
water crystals. He tested this by writing different words on
pieces of paper, taping them to glass jars full of water, and
then freezing them overnight. He labelled one jar of water
with the words 'thank you', another with the words 'love &
gratitude', and a third jar with the words 'you disgust me'.
These were the results:

'Thank you'   'Love & Gratitude'   'You disgust me'

Emoto found that it was not so much the words
themselves, but the intention behind them, that triggered
the molecular reaction in the water. He tried a similar
experiment using rice. He boiled a large amount of rice,
then separated it into two jars. The reason the rice was
boiled was to absorb all the water. On the first jar, Emoto
wrote the words *you fool*, and on the second, the words

thank you. Every day, he would spend a minute projecting hate on to the jar with the words *you fool,* and love on to the jar with the words *thank you.* He did this for a month then recorded the results. Here are the two jars at the end of the experiment:

'You fool'   *'Thank you'*

Emoto encouraged as many people as possible to replicate the rice experiment themselves, so they could see that he was not making it up. If this is what happens to boiled rice when intentions are projected on to it, just think of the implications this has for our own human body (which is around 70% water). Our thoughts and intentions have great power. If anything, Dr. Emoto's work teaches us the importance of love and appreciation in creating a better world.

One of the great marvels of quantum mechanics is the renowned double-slit experiment. In this experiment, electrons are fired out of a special cannon, one at a time, on to a screen. The experiment is set up in such a way as to leave a marking in the exact location the electron makes contact with the screen each time. There's a catch, though. Instead of firing the electrons directly on to the screen, they must first travel through one of two identical vertical slits.

After firing thousands of electrons, one at a time, through these two slits, we would logically expect to see two vertical lines on the screen at roughly the same height and distance apart as the two slits. Remarkably, this does not happen. Instead of the electrons behaving like particles, they behave like *waves*, and an interference pattern shows up on the screen (see diagram below).

Why do waves result in an interference pattern? One wave alone cannot create such a pattern, as there is nothing for it to interfere with. When the ripples of two waves collide, the peaks and troughs of both waves interact with each other, adding together in some cases and cancelling out in others, resulting in an interference pattern. How can there be two waves if each electron is being fired separately and passes through only one slit? The only explanation is that each electron passes through *both* slits at the same time, and interferes with itself.

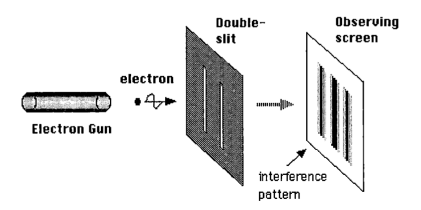

It gets weirder. Scientists wanted to see precisely what was happening at the subatomic level to explain this, so they set up a special camera pointed at the two slits. This time, when they ran the experiment, the electrons went back to behaving just like particles, and the pattern on the screen resembled two vertical lines! Instead of travelling through both slits at the same time, the electrons travelled through only one slit at a time. The simple act of *observing* the electrons meant that they changed their behaviour, as if aware something was watching. So the scientists decided to be cunning and unplugged the camera at its power source, while pretending to still be observing the electrons with the camera. The electrons went back to behaving like *waves* again, as if conscious of the fact that the camera was switched off. To this day, physicists have not been able to come up with a rational explanation for the double-slit experiment. At the quantum level, there appears to be some form of *intelligence* in matter. The double slit phenomenon validates what John Hagelin says about everything being 'just different ripples on a single ocean of existence'.

In his book, *The Sense of Being Stared At: And Other Aspects of the Extended Mind*, biologist Rupert Sheldrake remarks:

Matter is no longer the fundamental reality, as it was for old-style materialism. Fields and energy are now more fundamental than matter. The ultimate particles of matter have become vibrations of energy within fields. The boundaries of scientific 'normality' are shifting again with a dawning recognition of the reality of consciousness.

If thoughts and intention are energetic waves of vibration, as is suggested by the findings of Backster and Emoto, then the existence of telepathic phenomena would no longer seem like such a stretch of the imagination. Could it be that the potential for telepathy exists in all living organisms? If this ocean of consciousness that permeates all existence connects us all at the sub-nuclear level, then there also exists the potential for communication in all its forms. I'm not saying that we can just send messages with our mind across the universe to other galaxies, but the *potential* for telepathic communication likely exists.

According to Rupert Sheldrake, animals possess this ability to varying degrees, depending on the species. He documents many cases of pets picking up on their owner's intentions, absent of any physical cues or Pavlovian triggers. Sheldrake presents anecdotal evidence of cats who have anticipated a visit to the vet. He received testimonies from many cat owners describing their cats somehow knowing it was a vet day, before the owners had acted in any way that may have alluded to a vet visit. He mentions having heard specific accounts of cats going missing on vet days, as if they knew exactly what their owner's intentions were. To follow up on these claims, Sheldrake rang all the veterinary clinics in North London to ask them if they had many cancellations due to cats going missing at the time. 64 out of 65 clinics reported frequent cancellations due to missing cats. Another common phenomenon is that of dogs

knowing when they are going to be taken for a walk
outside of non-routine times. Sheldrake says he received
over a hundred accounts of dog owners who claimed their
dogs picked up on their intentions to take them for a walk,
even without any physical indicators.

An experiment was also carried out by Sheldrake with
a talking parrot named N'kisi, in which the parrot had to
guess the content of the photos its owner, Aimee, was
looking at. The photos had never been seen before, were
chosen at random by a third party and were each in their
own sealed envelope. Aimee was in a closed room 55 feet
away from N'kisi's cage. Two cameras recorded the
experiment from both the perspectives of N'kisi and
Aimee. On revealing a photo of a flower, N'kisi (unable to
see the photo) said, in broken English:

*You could put the, take the flower. You gotta go get camera, put
the flowers on now. That's a pic of flower.*

This is a parrot, mind you. I'm aware grammar and syntax
are lacking considerably. However, the *subject* of the photo
is still clearly the same subject the parrot is talking about.
Another photo was of a couple in skimpy swimwear
showing a lot of skin. The parrot remarked 'look at my
pretty naked body.' A third photo was of a man talking on
a mobile phone. N'kisi asked 'what'cha doing on the
phone?' followed by a series of mock answering machine
noises. This went on until Aimee had revealed a total of 71
photos. Of the 71 images, N'kisi had correctly identified 23
of them. That is a staggering degree of accuracy, seeing as

the parrot could not physically see any of the photos. The odds of achieving these results due to random chance would be millions, possibly even billions, to one. You have to remember, each photo could have been anything, and neither Sheldrake nor Aimee had any foreknowledge of the content of the photos. Sheldrake, who has researched animal telepathy for many years, asserts that the case study of N'kisi is the most extraordinary example of independent thought-recognition in an organism that he has ever seen firsthand.

In *The Sense of Being Stared At*, Sheldrake describes accounts of seemingly telepathic phenomena among humans. A prime example of this is when you are thinking of someone who then calls you on the telephone. There have been many documented cases of this. I for one have experienced this on more than one occasion, and I can tell you, it's a very strange feeling. A similar occurrence is when you are able to predict who is calling before you look at your phone, when you are not expecting their call.

Have you ever felt like someone was watching you from behind, and then turned around to find that someone *was* watching you from behind? This is not an uncommon experience. Sheldrake posits that this happens as a result of the watcher's attentional field:

Through focusing our attention on something at a distance it is as if our mind extends outwards to connect us with this distant object... this sense reveals that through the power of attention the mind is connected to the world beyond the body.

This could also be understood as the transference of energy. Have you ever heard the phrase 'energy flows where attention goes?' If you project your attention on to an object, you are sending out waves of vibration (in the form of energy), which are received by that object. Consider Masaru Emoto's rice experiment. Both containers of rice receive positive and negative waves of vibrational energy as attention is projected on to the two containers. Just because humans cannot visually perceive this energy doesn't mean it's not there. Humans cannot visually perceive a magnetic field but we know it's there because of its effect on various metallic objects. Thanks to Emoto's experiments we know that there must be some kind of energy transference that can be triggered purely by thought and intention.

People who are quick to denounce what we cannot see without adequate investigation seem to have forgotten that humans only perceive a very small percentage of the total visible spectrum... and that is only the visible spectrum that we know of at this point in our evolution. Sure, we know of infrared, ultraviolet, gamma rays, cosmic rays, microwaves, radio-waves (none of which humans can detect)... but that's only in *our* dimension. We have no clue what kinds of visible waveforms exist in other dimensions. We see only a tiny sliver of the full potential of conscious awareness. Many animals see what is invisible to the human eye. Cats can detect ultraviolet light, for instance. My point is, if we are to advance in our understanding of science, we must begin to take seriously that which we cannot see in a material sense.

The day science begins to study non-physical phenomena, it will make more progress in one decade than in all the previous centuries of its existence.

- Nikola Tesla

The knowledge that we are all part of the same whole within this infinite fabric of consciousness changes everything. Many of us have felt this intimacy between all organisms our whole lives. The Native American peoples, indigenous tribes of the world, yogis, and Buddhist monks have all known this connection for thousands of years. Most people are only just beginning to wake up to this truth, and now science is starting to embrace it. We exist as part of something that is much greater than our minds and much greater than our bodies. We are everything that exists in the universe. We are every animal, every tree, every cell, every star, every galaxy and everybody. The *self* is not *I*. The *self* is *we*; it is *us*; the *self* is the entire universe. You and I are of the same essence. To disrespect any living thing is to disrespect the essence we all belong to.

Knowing this, how can we possibly allow members of the human family to die needlessly or to suffer through oppression? In a world of plenty, how can we allow for so much starvation? How can we allow innocent men, women and children to be torn apart limb from limb in Gaza? We can no longer turn a blind eye to these atrocities; we can no longer stick our heads in the sand and pretend that we don't feel the suffering of our own people. It is not *their* suffering... it is *our* suffering. We have a tremendous responsibility to our fellow human beings, and to all life in the cosmos. It has come time to uphold that responsibility, and to teach the next generations to do the same. We need to awaken to our real power. We're brought up thinking that we're just a flesh vehicle with a name, a job and a bank balance. This is false. It is an *illusion*. We are not powerless to do anything outside of convention. We are not insignificant. We are not subservient to someone else's doctrines and someone else's ideas of how we must live out our lives. We are masters of our own destiny. Every single one of us has the power to bring about immense change. Every action we take affects everything else. When you drop the smallest stone into a pond, it creates a ripple. When you plant a seed, it one day becomes a towering tree. Every stone that is cast into a pond and every seed that is planted has the potential to alter the fabric of consciousness. This power is within us all.

We are now living in a critical time in human evolution. A great shift is taking place. The wheels of change are in motion. People are not falling for the same lies, the same broken promises, the same fake smiles and the same deception. We are starting to realise the game being played against us. We see how wars are fought for oil and profit. We see that the media do not represent our best interests. We see that we are being manipulated by a system that is supposed to serve us. Now, more than ever, we need to stand strong as one human family.

Bill Hicks famously said:

It's only a choice. No effort, no work, no job, no savings of money... a choice, right now, between fear and love. The eyes of fear want you to put bigger locks on your door, buy guns, close yourself off... the eyes of love instead see all of us as one.

He's right. It is a choice. We can transcend the paradigm of fear anytime we want. It is up to us to choose love instead. Love is the uniting force of all life. It is the ultimate healing power. The only way to save our species is to embrace this universal force of nature.

When the power of love overcomes the love of power, the world will know peace.

- Jimi Hendrix

A World Without Money

One cannot address the education system outside of the lens of the economic system. Take a look at our current paradigm of education. It revolves around moulding young people into obedient, unquestioning, productive workers. From a factory mentality, the system is churning out earners and consumers, so that the wheels will keep on turning, and so that the factory owners at the top are always satisfied. The world, as it stands, is a *business*. Education has been about preparing our young to enter this business. It is my firm standpoint that this business does not have humanity's best interests at heart. Instead of working towards the progression of our species, the sole aim of this economic model has been self-preservation. We are not working for the common good. We are working so that the rich and powerful become more-so. We're running this giant machine that isn't doing anything except protecting its own existence.

Even though money may seem like a necessary part of our lives, it is both a tool for our enslavement and detrimental to our evolution. When you look at most of the big problems facing the world today, money is at the root of them all. Poverty, homelessness, war, crime, unemployment, poor healthcare, pollution, child labor, deforestation, the elimination of the middle class...

Industry is about profit, when it should be about progress. As long as profit-based industries exist, we will never have the best technology, the most innovative solutions to global problems, and the highest mental and physical health standards. Why? It's actually quite simple when you take a step back from it all and consider how industries maintain their empires. I touched on this in Chapter 7, but it needs reiterating. Let's use the cancer industry again as an example.

Cancer is a multibillion dollar industry, and prices for chemotherapy and radiotherapy are sky high. Most people can't afford these treatments without going into significant debt. On top of this, there's only a 2% success rate, and even then, there's a chance the cancer could return at a later time. Still, people line up for the treatments, exposing their bodies to immense amounts of radiation in the hope of survival... and the industry is raking it in. Along comes something like cannabis oil, which through an enormous body of anecdotal evidence, has been proven to be extremely effective in the treatment of serious cancers and most other physical illnesses. Does the cancer industry embrace such a cure? No. If they did, they would go out of business. They know full well such a cure exists and continue to deny its effectiveness. The cancer industry is not interested in a cure they cannot make money out of. If you think they really care about us, think again. They are only in it for the bottom line.

The energy industry (the most powerful industry in the world) has no interest in free and abundant energy for all. If energy were to be decentralised or stripped of its price tag, they would not have a business. So it is in their interests to meter all energy usage and to regulate the price. It is also in their interests to suppress new energy technologies that threaten the survival of their empire.

The cosmetics industry needs people (particularly women) to be ashamed of their natural bodies in order to turn a profit. If women decided they were happy with the way they are and didn't need to cover their faces and bodies in makeup, moisturisers, exfoliants, lipstick, mascara, and celebrity-endorsed perfumes, then the cosmetics industry would not survive. This industry, along with the fashion industry, the hair-care industry and the fitness industry, all rely on us being insecure with ourselves. They don't just rely on our insecurities, they go out of their way to *make* us insecure through marketing campaigns and advertising strategies.

Most of the products on the market are designed not to last, or to be replaced by a new model in a couple of years. This is called *planned obsolescence*, and we find it happening everywhere. A perfect example of this is the iPhone. Have you noticed how every model since the very first iPhone has been flawed in some way, or was very easily made redundant by the next one? We're now up to iPhone 6, which (surprise, surprise) is embarrassingly bendable. Do people really think an empire worth billions of dollars would be so incompetent as to overlook such a glaring flaw in the design process? Apple isn't stupid. They didn't build their empire by accident. They've just made the iPhone 7 that much more attractive when they release it, and thus stand to make more money.

I've singled out Apple here, but the reality is that this is happening all over the market. Just consider this. If a company designed the best product possible that didn't break, and would never need to be replaced, how would they make their money two years later when everyone has moved on? They wouldn't, and their business would cease to exist. Under a profit-based model of industry, the best in human innovation does not provide a sustainable business model. Therefore, real human progress is not possible under the current system.

The single most important reason to work towards a moneyless society is the fact that our economy functions out of *debt*. As discussed in Chapter 2, the Federal Reserve system, and indeed all central banks in existence, create money out of nothing and then loan it out with *interest*. There is never enough money in circulation to pay back the interest, so our governments have to keep loaning the money from the central banks, accruing more debt. The banks own the money supply and therefore have power over our governments. What happens to the global economy when the Federal Reserve wants its $18 trillion back?

Society functions out of debt too. We think going to University or College is this huge privilege, and that we'll be better off with a higher education. Instead, what we end up with is a piece of paper and a mountain of debt. Student loans keep most tertiary students in chains for the rest of their lives. The real insanity of the matter is that we enter higher education to get a job in order to pay off the debt we're drowning in as a result of our higher education. That's the reality. It's absolute madness. Then once we get a real job the banks push their 'no limit' credit cards on us. Many people fall into this trap and cannot get out of it. The majority of people cannot own their own home without taking out a mortgage from the banks. Even then, it's not their home is it? The banks own it because the occupant owes the bank money. All our lives we are forced into debt. Very few of us manage to dodge the debt trap. It's everywhere and it keeps us enslaved to the monetary system.

Hypothetically, let's say that we abolished *interest*, took the power of money creation away from the banks and gave it to our governments, establishing an honest monetary system. Let's also say that somehow we were able to wipe the debt clock clean and hold the bankers accountable for the scam they have been running on the people, thus freeing the global economy from debt. To many, this would be a sufficient outcome for the world. To me, it would be a step in the right direction. However, the distribution of wealth would not change, and neither would most of the world's problems. The world would still be a business that puts profit before prosperity. Human suffering would continue. The destruction of our environment would continue... and we would continue to be at war with our own species.

Take money out of the equation and all of a sudden we have a completely different ball game. I believe we need to gradually transition to a moneyless society in order to evolve. The writing is on the wall. If we do not change our ways, we will destroy ourselves. We cannot afford to keep supporting this twisted system. It is exploiting us and holding us back.

So what would a moneyless society look like and how would it work?

Ubuntu Contributionism

Ubuntu Contributionism is the creation of Michael Tellinger, a South African man with a dream for a world of unity and abundance. The word 'Ubuntu' represents an African philosophy based on human kindness and the spirit of community. In English, it more or less translates to 'I am because we are.'

In the words of Michael Tellinger:

The UBUNTU Contributionism philosophy is largely based on the ancient tribal structures of the African people and many other native tribes of the world – with adaptations for our times and people accustomed to certain levels of technology of today. For thousands of years, the native people of the world lived in united tribal communities, in harmony with mother Earth. But our society has been segregated and separated on so many levels that we hardly understand the word 'unity' any more.

The UBUNTU model will break down the overcrowded urban areas allowing people to recreate a unified society consisting of smaller harmonious communities, where people can live by choice rather than forced into economic dependency and servitude.

The UBUNTU model restores this harmonious balance between the people and the land, providing abundance for all, because it is an environment which allows its people to contribute their natural talents and acquired skills to the greater benefit of everyone in the community. An environment where their talents are celebrated and supported on every level, at every age.

This applies to all areas of our society; from science, technology, agriculture, manufacture, health, education, housing, to every other area that is not deemed to be financially viable under the present capitalistic system.

Tellinger bases an Ubuntu society on five basic principles:

1) No money
2) No barter
3) No trade
4) Everyone contributes their natural talents or acquired skills for the greater benefit of all in their community

5) All contributions have equal value for the community

Contributionism is centred around cooperation instead of competition. Right now, we live in a pyramidal, hierarchical structure where the few dominate the many. In an Ubuntu society, complete abundance will be available to all who contribute. No one will have access to more than anyone else. The model ensures that there is no barrier in the way of progress, and that creation is only limited by the imagination.

Governance

Each individual community will appoint a Council of Elders made up of thirteen people that have the full trust and respect of the community at large. They are not self-appointed, they are entirely chosen by the people of the community based on their integrity and wisdom. The Council of Elders in each community will not necessarily be made up of older people. One person from the Council of Elders will be appointed as the spokesperson for the council, but all members will govern their communities equally. The Council of Elders will make decisions to benefit the needs of the community, initiate the implementation of new ideas or projects, and function transparently. The people will have full access to the council every day and be able to raise any concerns. It will be free from bureaucratic control and red tape, as there will be no need for them. The Council for each community will be voted on by the people each year or as long as deemed necessary.

How will people contribute?

The beauty of this kind of a society is that it values everyone's individual passions, talents and skills no matter what they are. If you're an artist, you will be acknowledged, valued and respected by the community. Same if you are a fisherman, a writer, an engineer, a teacher, an entertainer... every single person's passions and skillsets will be valued and appreciated equally. No longer will passionate artisans have to work as receptionists for corporations or as bank tellers. Everybody will be able to fully embrace their passion without having to worry about not making any money. Money no longer exists in such a society.

How Contributionism works is that every person above the age of sixteen contributes to their community for 3 hours per day, five days a week, doing what they *love* doing and do best! On top of this, they contribute to community projects for 2-3 hours per week, to ensure that all the needs of the community are met. That's a maximum of 18 hours per week for everybody doing what makes you feel happy! How can anyone argue with that? Provided everyone is a contributor, everything will be made available to everyone to access, everyone will have a good home, and everyone will have an abundance of resources at their finger-tips. Money is no longer a factor in production, so there is no limit on what can be produced.

Let me give you an example of how this works. I might elect teaching as my passion or skillset. I get to teach kids for three hours per day, five days a week, helping them to discover their own passions and talents and to discover what life is all about. Then I spend another two to three hours contributing to a project which benefits the entire community. The rest of the time I can spend however I choose. The reality is that families will have so much more time to spend with each other and work will no longer be a preoccupation to stop people from doing what they want to do with their life.

Laws

All laws and rules under the current Capitalist system will be abolished and new laws and rules will be written based on the inalienable rights of the people and the needs of the community. This will be decided by the people of each community and enacted by the Council of Elders.

According to Tellinger, all communities would begin with three basic laws:

1) Do not kill or cause anyone harm
2) Do not steal or take that which is not yours
3) Conduct yourself honestly and honourably in all that you do and say

Beyond this, each community will develop its own new set of laws based on the needs of the whole. People who greatly abuse the rules of the community will be given the opportunity for rehabilitation, or failing that will be asked to leave the community. Communities will be interconnected and conduct themselves in alignment with one another, so as to be mutually of benefit to one another.

Living Situation

In an Ubuntu world, no one is homeless. Every single person will be able to have a home built for them by the best architects and builders in the community. They can have customised furniture constructed by the best carpenters and craftspeople as well. Everyone is allocated land by the community and Council of Elders, based on their needs and their labour of love. For instance, farmers will need an appropriate amount of land for producing food for the community. All requests for housing would be considered within reason. Requests that go far beyond necessity would likely not be carried out. That means mansions or castles would not likely be an option. Again, this would be subject to the rules and laws of the community as decided by the people.

Technology and Advancement

Moving into the Ubuntu system does not mean going back to the dark ages and living as our tribal ancestors once lived. It will be quite the opposite. Money is actually stopping us from progressing. Take MagLev trains for example. We have the vision, the design and the expertise between all the people of the planet to build a safe global MagLev transport network, we just don't have the money to put up. It's not politically and economically viable to get such a network up and running as soon as possible. Remove money from the equation and all of a sudden there is no cost for such a job, and it doesn't take fifty years to implement. Anything becomes possible and we are only limited by what we can envision; no economic hurdles, no bureaucratic hurdles, no political hurdles, and no technological hurdles. We will be able to travel to the other side of the world in a couple of hours, be able to innovate at a level beyond anything we can imagine in the current system, and perhaps even reach new planets, new galaxies and new dimensions. If humanity can evolve, there is no reason why these things will not be in our reach one day.

We will be at the forefront of energy technology, implementing sustainable and renewable energy solutions throughout every community. There will be a great deal of research into new energy devices that tap into the zero-point field, as well as alternate fuel for transport, so that all of our energy needs are catered for in the most efficient and environmentally friendly ways imaginable. Under the Ubuntu model, we will be able to automate as many monotonous and lacklustre jobs as possible, while also ensuring that the maintenance of such robots is an automated process as well. This will free everyone up to contribute only in ways that are pleasing to the soul and allow for a much higher quality of life for all. I cannot stress this enough - automation will be the death of the capitalist model. Automation leads to unemployment which leads to less spending which leads to economic collapse. Take money away and automation takes away the worst jobs, increases productivity, and frees up humanity to live the best lives possible.

Education

Tellinger's philosophy for education is for children to *learn by doing*. Instead of being cooped up in classrooms all day and learning theoretical concepts from textbooks for the most part, he advocates for an entirely new approach to education; one that focuses on learning in a diverse range of environments.

The normal classroom is a synthetic environment separated from the natural processes that take place in a myriad of things that people do. You cannot effectively learn how to make cheese in a classroom – you cannot learn how to build a free-energy machine in a classroom. In fact, there is very little that we can truly learn in classrooms. Each skill must be experienced in its own environment to be truly absorbed by those learning it.
- Michael Tellinger

In an Ubuntu society, education will have a much larger focus on practical life skills. Specialist teachers will be appointed by their community and Council of Elders, based on their knowledge, expertise and passion for teaching. A huge problem with education all over the world is that vast numbers of teachers are underqualified for their chosen discipline. As the public teaching wage is so low in most countries, most 'master' teachers are drawn towards private tutoring where they stand to make a great deal more money for sharing their expertise. Children are missing out on learning from the best because of this failing system. Only teachers who are masters in their craft or discipline will be chosen to teach the children of Ubuntu communities.

There will be a greater emphasis on learning about nature and the importance of showing respect to the earth and everything in it. Wherever possible, learning about nature will take place *in* the natural environment, where children can experience a real connection to their world, instead of looking at books and computer screens.

Children will be encouraged to come up with creative solutions to the challenges of the community that will be run past the Council of Elders. They will play a more active role in their community, and their input will be valued and respected.

Though Tellinger's vision for education and my own vision for education are structured quite differently, our philosophies and principles are much the same, as you will discover in the following chapter. I believe my model for education would work well in an Ubuntu society. For a full and in-depth description of Tellinger's educational vision, I urge you to read his book, *Ubuntu Contributionism: A Blueprint for Human Prosperity.*

Transitioning to Ubuntu

Like all change, transitioning to a world without money is likely to be a gradual, evolutionary process. There is already a shift in the global consciousness happening right now. People are awakening from the stupor of their day to day lives now that many of the world's problems are beginning to arrive at their own doorstep.

The first step in making this a reality is to establish the very first functioning Ubuntu community. Michael Tellinger is well on the way to doing this already. He has acquired a community hall, community kitchen, gymnasium, outdoor recreational area and a fish farm in his South African town of Waterval Boven. He has the support of many of the local people and is also receiving help from all over the world.

Tellinger is a member of the South African Ubuntu Party which intends to get its message across via a political platform. The movement has spread far and wide, and has garnered coordinators and representatives from 77 countries.

Once the community kitchen is fully operational, the plan is to provide food for the homeless people, the orphaned, and anyone else who contributes to their community projects. Tellinger believes that when he has the trust of the local people, word will spread and others will become interested in the projects. Positive change begins with love and kindness. From there, he wants to establish a people's bank account to keep the community's money separate from the commercial banks. All money that goes into the account will go towards projects to make the community less dependent on money. If Ubuntu communities are to become fully independent, it is necessary to work with money in the early stages. Tellinger acknowledges that the initial stages will be a huge uphill battle, but is determined to persevere at all costs.

When the community can produce an abundance of food and other goods for a fraction of the price in neighbouring towns, they will allow people from the neighbouring towns to buy their produce for very little money. Tellinger believes this will leave neighbouring towns with no choice but to adopt the same model and start their own Ubuntu communities. When people keep continuing to buy their food at a fraction of the cost from an Ubuntu community, other businesses will be forced to adapt. This is how Contributionism picks up speed and activates all the surrounding towns. From there, it's simply a matter of *the domino effect* coming into play.

Frequently Asked Questions

1. *Who is going to shovel the crap?*

In the beginning stages, people will need to share the dirty jobs as part of their 3 hours a week of community contributionism. This is a small price to pay per week in order to establish abundance and foster communities that prosper. Those jobs can be automated in time, as machines will run right around the clock and be programmed to maintain themselves. No one will be forced against their will to do these jobs, but the benefits of Ubuntu communities will only be available to those who contribute.

2. *If everything is free, can I have ten mansions and fifty Ferraris?*

Accumulating lavish material possessions is a way to parade one's social status in front of friends and neighbours. Social class doesn't exist in a Contributionist system as everyone has the same access to abundance as everyone else. If you have ten mansions, you will have no more power than anyone else, and will be impressing no one. It's likely that such people will not be popular for taking up unnecessary plots of land, and the system will not reward this behaviour, unlike Capitalism.

3. *Why should I give up all the things I've worked so hard for all my life?*

You will not be giving up anything. You will have access to everything you could ever want or need in such a society. Material possessions will not have the same value in Ubuntu communities as they do in the current system.

4. *Is this not just another form of Communism?*

This is *nothing* like Communism. Communism is an ideology that functions on money. Communism is a centralised system like Capitalism. Contributionism on the

other hand, consists of interconnected, but independent,
self-sustaining communities within a decentralised system.
Money doesn't exist in such a world.

   5. *People are inherently lazy. When given the option, they
      will sit around all day and do nothing.*

Most of us do work that we hate in order to survive.
Laziness is a consequence of Capitalism. We are not hard-
wired to be lazy. We only behave this way when we feel
defeated, powerless and lack self-worth. These things are a
symptom of the machine and the rat race we are forced to
run. More than anything, we are hard-wired to create.
From the moment we're born, we love to create... until the
standardized education system gets a hold of us and drains
us of this most natural drive. In an Ubuntu society, people
will be able to create to their heart's content as part of their
labour of love.

This model is not perfect. It has its bumps and creases. Like
all new systems, it will have problems, many unforeseeable
in the beginning. That said, it is an *out* for humanity. It may
be our best shot at ascending to the next phase of our
evolution and repairing the damage we have done to our
fellow man and our planet. I understand if it doesn't click
just yet, but give it time. Don't rush to condemn it. It is not
a threat to the layperson's existence. Those who believe
they have more power than everyone else will likely see it
as a threat as it takes away their perceived power and
starves their ego. As far as I am concerned, there is no place

in the world for ego-driven power. Those who have opted to place their own profit over their own humanity will be the losers in this shift, and rightfully so. Justice must be delivered to the psychopaths who have abused their power time and time again. The enslavement of humanity has to come to an end.

There is so much more to the Contributionism model that I cannot go into detail about here. I urge you to read Tellinger's book and watch his presentations on YouTube. Check the *References* section at the back for more information.

The Venus Project

I want to also draw attention to another big idea based on a world without money called *The Venus Project*. It is the brainchild of a man named Jacque Fresco, and works on the system of a *Resource Based Economy (RBE)*. Fresco says that the current system we live in manufactures scarcity through the distribution of wealth, and it is this manufactured scarcity that causes most of the world's problems.

It was living through the 1929 Great Depression that helped shape my social conscience. During this time, I realised the earth was still the same place. Manufacturing plants were still intact and resources were still there but people didn't have the money to buy the products. I felt the rules of the game we play by were obsolete and insufficient.

- Jacque Fresco

In his research centre in Venus, California, Fresco came up with a complete blueprint for his vision of a Resource Based Economy that eliminates the concept of scarcity. In order to manage the sustainable and efficient distribution of the earth's resources, a computer database would be set up to determine where resources are needed and in what quantity.

Communities would be built in such a way as to achieve the greatest possible efficiency from the smallest use of space, while maintaining high standards of living for everyone. Fresco's architectural designs are less blocky and regimented than we have today, and instead feature rounded edges and curves like something out of a high-budget science fiction movie. Though his concepts are highly futuristic, they are no doubt easily within our reach.

People would be given the option to live in individual homes or high-rise apartment buildings, with a community emphasis on apartment living. In order to eliminate monotonous and soulless work, as many jobs would be automated as possible, freeing up humanity to get the most out of their lives. As for the jobs that wouldn't be automated, people would be happy to do those jobs provided they are meaningful to their lives. Think about the great inventors and explorers of our past. They didn't invent and explore so they could have the money to survive. They did so because they had an insatiable curiosity and drive. They believed that humanity was capable of greatness and spent their lives trying to prove it. If we take money away, it is still in our nature to strive towards progress. For many, human progress is a worthy lifelong pursuit. I did not write this book to survive. I am not trying to change the education system to feed, clothe and shelter myself. I am doing it all because I want to see a better world and it gives meaning to my life to work for the greater benefit of all humankind. Prior to writing this book I was a semi-successful voice-over artist with a nice little nest egg. Now, as a consequence of devoting my time and energy to this book, I am broke and barely scraping together my rent. That should give you a clear picture of what money means to me.

In a Resource Based Economy, the focus would be on technology and innovation. Fresco says that such a society would not be an *established* society like the one we have, but an *emergent* one, that is ever-changing, and always growing towards something better. The environment would be treated with a newfound respect, and cities would provide many places for nature to flourish within them.

Fresco advocates for a scientific government on the basis that scientists and engineers are better equipped to solve the world's problems than any kind of political government. He stresses that a scientific government would not be given control over laws, regulations and the distribution of resources, but only be in charge of technological progress. Instead of making new laws to stop a problem from occurring, Fresco promotes a practical approach to solving the problems so that they don't happen again. He believes there are very few laws that could not be replaced by technological solutions. As for control of the resources, that would be managed by an intricate computer network. The world's environmental problems would be solved through the application of renewable energy solutions such as solar, wind, wave, tidal and above all, geothermal. Cars would all be running on electric power and all public transport would be replaced by a global Maglev train network that would eventually utilise evacuated tube transport technology. You would be able to go from New York to Beijing in two hours. The same could easily be achieved in an Ubuntu society as well, so this is not an advantage that The Venus Project has over Contributionism.

If any of this is confusing or if you are concerned these ideas are without merit, please watch Jacque Fresco's documentary titled *Paradise or Oblivion.* There is a web address in the *References* section. Most, if not all of your questions will be answered by watching that documentary. If I could compare Ubuntu with The Venus Project, I would say that Ubuntu has more of a lean towards *stronger human connection* and The Venus Project has more of a lean towards *technological achievement.* To me, I believe that if we begin a new society that does not have its core focus on compassion, love and higher consciousness, we will again lose sight of what it means to be truly human. Though I do not want to take away from the hard work and heroism of Jacque Fresco, I have more faith in a Contributionist society purely because of its humanitarian philosophy. To me, it would be a mistake to seek technological progress *before* we have learned to live in harmony with one another on this planet. Once we have solved the problem of peaceful cohabitation, then we can bring humanity forward, as one family, to the next stage of our technological evolution.

It is clear to me that public sentiment towards our current system is rapidly changing. We are getting sick and tired of the war, the political deception and the human suffering under this out-dated model of Capitalism. Automation is naturally on the rise because it is more profitable for industries to hire robots instead of humans. However, Big Business does not seem to realise that by automating their jobs, they are actually bringing about their own demise, since jobless humans do not have money to feed into circulation. Capitalism is phasing itself out and cannot continue for much longer. A new system is called for, and with it, a new education system. Let us use this opportunity to free ourselves from the chains of a monetary system. We don't need money to prosper in unity and abundance. We have the facility, the technology, the resourcefulness, the wisdom and the expertise to create a world that works for everyone completely free of financial enslavement.

The Six Dimension Model

We know the current education system is broken. I daresay you wouldn't be reading this book right now if you didn't think education needed to undergo some big changes. Einstein once said, *'We cannot solve our problems with the same level of thinking that created them.'*

He was dead right. We cannot repair the education system by looking at it from the same lens we have always viewed it. We must rethink the entire paradigm.

This isn't an easy task for anyone. After all, we grew up with the industrial model and it's all we've ever known. When you're a five year old child, and you don the uniform and schoolbag for the first time, you don't realise what you're entering into, nor do you have any say in the matter. You just do what you're told because school is a normal part of life. You never really stop to question the way that your teachers teach all through your schooling years. After all, they're adults, and they're probably smarter than you - they must be, right?

You become accustomed to ringing bells, to regimented schedules, to spending most of your time indoors, and to doing what you are told. It's all just a part of getting ready to be a grown-up one day. Once it has become so deeply ingrained in your programming, it's hard to question it.

It took an awakening moment of clarity for me to realise that there was a better way. I decided that rather than trying to fix what we already had, it would be more effective to wipe the slate clean and build a new model from the ground up. In order to come up with the initial blueprint for a new system, a redefinition of terms was necessary. The Oxford dictionary defines education as *the process of receiving or giving systematic instruction.* This definition is false, it is damaging, and it is quite possibly the reason critical thinking is such a rare thing in today's society. It does not account for the mind's ability to teach itself. When it really comes down to it, education is *learning for life.* That's how I choose to define it. The biggest question inside a child's mind is, *what is this thing we call life?* It is up to the education system to give children the tools they need to find a meaningful answer to that question. Of course, the answer varies for everyone, but isn't that the beauty of it?

With the terms redefined, I then had to work out the most important things a child would need to learn to enrich that child's life. So I came up with *The Six Dimension Model* (See diagram opposite). It is important to note that there is a great deal of overlap within these six dimensions. Certain concepts, skills and methods fall under more than one dimension. All of the dimensions, *self-discovery, inquiry, sustainability, innovation, communication* and *empathy*, should be treated equally. Though some of these may jump out more to you than others, I do not attempt to rank them in any way. We all have our own opinions as to what areas we believe are more or less important in education. There is no hierarchical structure to this model. The main aim of this approach is to bring much-needed balance to the education system and to make sure that children are not alienated by it in any way, shape or form.

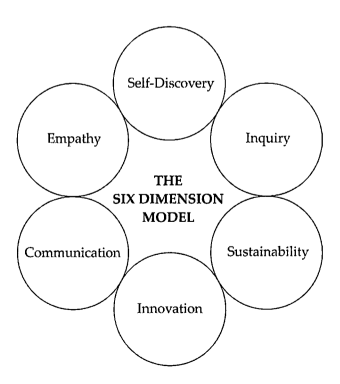

This is not a perfect system. I don't think there is such a thing. I completely understand if people have disagreements with any of my thoughts and ideas for these six dimensions. I would expect few people to agree with everything. I am a proponent of collaboration and open-sourcing, so it is my wish to give this model to the world for everyone to work on and to make better. I am hoping to start an online hub where I can share the core ideas of this model and provide a community where anyone can contribute to this work-in-progress. If we all put our hearts and our minds together, and unite for the greater good, we can turn this system into something truly awe-inspiring that works for everyone. I do not wish to be selfish, to trademark this model, to copyright it, to keep it to myself, to call it exclusively *mine*...

I am giving it to you, the reader, to do whatever you can to help make this a reality.

SELF-DISCOVERY

The first of these six dimensions focuses on helping children find what it is that excites them, what makes them feel alive, what their talents are, what their interests are, and who they are underneath any layers of social superficiality. To be able to give children the opportunity to discover what their heart is yearning for, we have to ensure that as many avenues of discovery as possible are available to them.

Aesthetics

Aesthetics is the name I have given to *the arts*, as I feel it better encapsulates the nature of these creative pursuits. The arts deserve to be recognised as manifestations of beauty and not just aspects of cultural expression. In this new model, music, dance, theatre, poetry, visual art, film-making, photography, culinary arts, pottery, craft and writing will all be available for children to learn and specialise in. Anything else that should have made this list will be available as well. It's high time we gave the right-brained learners the chance to really shine.

Children who take on aesthetic pursuits will not be pushed into academic pursuits beyond primary level. They will be encouraged to take part in a wide range of learning experiences outside of aesthetic endeavours, but never forced against their will. Teachers of aesthetics will be of the highest calibre in their field of expertise. Children who learn from masters are much more likely to achieve mastery themselves. Workshops of varying lengths will take place in the child's chosen discipline so they can have the opportunity to bond with that pursuit more closely and strengthen their talents that much more.

Sports and Outdoor Activities

Likewise, children should be able to have the same access to sporting and outdoor interests as they would with avenues of artistry. I believe the focus needs to begin to shift from competitive sports to collaborative sports and other non-competitive sports. I acknowledge that some humans learn competition from a very early age, so I don't think competitive sports can be ruled out completely for quite some time.

The only reason I believe this shift should start to occur is because competition breeds a winner/loser mentality. Competition causes division and leads to hierarchical structures of value. It is because of competitive attitudes that we have arrived at such a state in our world where we walk past homeless people in the street without as much as a glance. That said, I don't think humanity would be ready to wipe out competition in sports. It is the kind of thing that will be phased out over a period of generations, and it will occur naturally as part of human evolution. A whole new range of sports will be invented over time that focus on working together to achieve an aim other than beating an opponent. For the purposes of this model, competitive sports will be available, and schools will look at fostering respect and good sportsmanship on the field.

Martial arts will be available as part of this area of education, with the focus on self-defensive and non-aggressive disciplines such as aikido. Like aesthetics teachers, all sports and outdoor activities teachers will be highly skilled and highly trained in their chosen field.

Creative Play

For children in the primary years, creative play will be an essential part of their development. A certain amount of time each day will be dedicated to providing children with all the resources necessary to manifest their spontaneity in the world. Pencils, markers, crayons, paints, paper, materials, scissors, glue, building blocks, shapes, computer art programs... anything that allows children to express their creative instincts. Even musical instruments could be made available to children in a separate room or with headphones. Children will have the choice of creating on their own or collaborating in pairs or small groups. Teachers will use this time to interact on an individual level with each and every child and to attempt to connect to each child on a personal level. They will enquire about each child's creations, identify areas in which the children appear driven, and nurture their interests. Teachers will give encouragement, support and guidance to children so they can be helped towards what naturally excites them.

On top of creative play, teachers will regularly engage in games with the children in the earlier years. I have seen, through first-hand experience, how games are able to activate a child's mind and stimulate the brain in preparation for educational learning. Children who take part in a five minute game before a numeracy lesson are much more switched on and ready to engage in the lesson than when there is no icebreaker game. When I was in Kathmandu, I played games with the 6th Form kids and I'd never seen so many smiles in one room. It seemed like it was the first time they had played games during school time, and they looked like they came alive all of a sudden. Even the assistant principal looked like he was having fun. Kids need to have fun in schools. It helps them learn and it strengthens the teacher/student bond. Games should not stop after childcare, crèche and kinder. Kids need to be kids!

Meditation

It is my hope that every school under this model will take part in meditation classes two or three times a week at all age levels. Meditation should begin as early as the first year of school, but would vary greatly as the children grow and develop. In the earliest year of school, ten minutes is all the time needed to spend meditating. As very young children tend to be fidgety and have trouble switching off when left to their own devices, these children will learn through a guided process. Similar to being read a story, the meditation instructor will lead the children through a simulated journey of the imagination, using calming music and the sounds of nature to provide greater context to the experience.

They can choose to meditate in any position that is most comfortable to them, whether sitting cross-legged or lying with their head supported by a cushion. This method of meditating is mainly to get the youngest children to reach a deep state of relaxation and to learn to be comfortable in their own space.

As they get older they will transition to Zen meditation which is about focusing in on the breath. They will learn to sit in a cross-legged position (no need to sit in a lotus position) and meditate in complete silence for no more than twenty minutes. This should be a part of their schooling all the way up until the age of sixteen - the age I believe traditional schooling should end. For children who are strongly resistant to this practice, other options will be available to them. It is my hope that children who practise meditation from an early age will grow to love it and experience profound benefits from it.

I credit meditation greatly with discovering the path that resonated with me. I was able to reach such deep states of relaxation and able to experience such rich feelings of euphoria and bliss, that it made me far less irritable and edgy in the days following a meditation session. I remember how at ease I was when I first began meditating, and how I didn't have to wrack my brain to find the words I was looking for. They flowed from the tongue naturally. Instead of losing my cool when a car suddenly pulled out in front of me, it didn't seem to faze me at all. People would look at me differently, like they could feel how comfortable, confident and at peace I was with myself. All my cares melted away. It put me more in tune with my own desires and elevated my conscious awareness of everything in the world. It gave me a renewed appreciation of nature and of the birds chirping outside my bedroom window. I felt what it was like to be truly human and to feel alive... really alive.

Through meditation, children will be able to experience clarity of mind. They will develop stronger neural pathways and their creative potential will increase tenfold. It will bring them closer to their sense of *self*. They will connect with the infinite stream of consciousness that binds all of existence as one, and have a sense of *knowing* what is deeply intuitive to their own being. Meditation will assist greatly in unearthing their passions, dreams and deep desires in life. They will grow up to become better human beings - I have no doubt of that.

INQUIRY

If we are to create a new education system, it must be one that teaches children *how* to think instead of *what* to think. They need to learn how to activate their minds instead of being treated as consumers of information. Inquiry must be at the heart of a new model. Learning should take place through the investigative process wherever applicable, and children should be encouraged to question *everything*.

History

What they teach in schools is always someone else's version of history. In many cases, it is a propagandized account of what happened, written by those who wish to keep people ignorant of the facts. How can we teach one version of history when we cannot discern the number of truths and untruths within a single narrative? How can we tell our children that events took place in a certain way when there is also a body of evidence to suggest it did not take place in that way? We cannot teach history this way without indoctrinating the future generations.

Instead of teaching a single version of events as the truth, students will also look at alternative explanations for those events in history. These alternative explanations should not be treated as 'alternative', but instead as accounts from a different perspective. The teacher's role in history class will be to briefly outline each version of events and then to provide the children with all the tools and resources necessary for them to investigate the evidence

themselves. Children will be encouraged to look at all the
evidence from every angle – through newspaper articles,
video footage, independent media outlets, witness
testimony, government statements, leaked documents –
anywhere that evidence can be gathered. They will be
asked to weigh all the evidence and to reach their own
conclusions, whatever those conclusions may be. It does
not matter if children reach different conclusions. This is to
be embraced. It means that they are not prone to the
dangers of Orwellian *groupthink* and have full mastery over
their own minds. By learning in this way, children will be
constantly honing their critical thinking skills and become
much better at discerning information. They will not
blindly accept what they are being told by anyone,
regardless of whether that information is true or not. They
will learn to conduct their own inquiries and to base their
judgment on all the facts available. The truth is rarely black
and white. Children must be able to decide for themselves
what feels right to them.

Philosophy

Students at all levels will take place in healthy
philosophical discourse with their teachers and peers. This
practice will get them to look beyond the spheres of their
daily lives and to take in *the big picture.* So often in today's
society we are preoccupied with work, with our families,
with the relentless pursuit of money and success, with
entertainment and with our social lives. We seldom, if at
all, take the time to step back from it all and consider our

place in the universe, or contemplate the nature of reality. I'm not saying that we always need to be in a state of inquisitiveness and rumination, but it's necessary at least *some* of the time in order to grasp the fullness of life. How are we supposed to appreciate our very existence if we don't take stock of things from a greater perspective? Philosophy is a remarkably important thing to teach as it shows our children that it is OK to think differently... it is OK to have a different view of the world... it is OK to challenge conventions. In fact, it is necessary to do so. The way philosophy is taught should be such that it excites as many students as possible. For philosophy to be effective, it need only ask big questions - questions which are of interest to an inquisitive mind. It does not matter that there are no clear answers to those questions, because the point of such a study is to get people *thinking*. A child who learns how to think will be better equipped than any number of high-achieving children who passively accept what they are told.

Abolishment of Religious Education

Religious doctrines will have no place in this education model. If you wish to teach your children to worship a deity outside of school, it is within your rights to do so. Though I am against parents who think it is OK to push religion on to their children at their most vulnerable, suggestible stages of life, I am more concerned about this indoctrination happening in the education system. I don't care whether you're Christian, Muslim, Jewish, Hindu,

Jesuit or Roman Catholic... religion should not, and will not, be a part of a new education system. To those who are religious, I am not insulting your faith. I am not against your faith. What I am, however, is strongly in favour of letting children make up their own minds when they are of a maturity to process information critically. I went to a private school which just so happened to be Anglican as well. A great many of the children were non-religious. Yet we had religious education (or R.E.) classes in primary school and in high school, as well as weekly chapel services. During these services we would be forced to sing Christian hymns, forced to read the Lord's prayer aloud and forced to listen to sermons. Those who didn't join in during the hymns were reprimanded.

I remember sitting in religious education class listening to our school chaplain prattle on about Abraham and Joseph, and thinking, 'why do I have to learn this crap?' Many years later I am grateful for having not swallowed it willingly. However, I regret having so much of my life taken from me due to religious education. No child deserves to be put through these doctrines in school. It is the right of every child to choose whether he or she would like to be a part of a religion.

Even if religion was voluntary in schools, which religion do you teach? If you teach one religion, you discount all the others. I can't even count the number of religions on both of my hands, so teaching all religions wouldn't work either. Religious education must be abolished from schooling altogether. That said, there is nothing wrong with discussing religion as part of a study of philosophy. There is much to learn from such a discourse, and it is to be encouraged.

The Socratic Method

The role of the teacher will shift in a new education system. Instead of being an authority on knowledge and information, teachers will mostly act as *facilitators*, and the real teachers will be the students themselves. Our minds are not passive containers for storing as much information as they can hold. They are tools for creation. One of the most beautiful and profound abilities of the human brain is the ability to create unique thoughts that have never before been created. Somehow, human beings can turn *nothing* into *something* merely by activating the neuronal impulses in parts of the brain. Yet our education system largely ignores this miraculous trait of our nature and sees the brain as a sponge. In this way, students are only learning what their teachers want them to learn in any given lesson. That is why in western education, lessons are planned according to statements of specific 'learning objectives'. If a child achieves these learning objectives, they fit the mould the system wants.

The Socratic Method flips this on its head. Lessons take on the form of an open dialogue where the learning objective is always *to get the students to think for themselves.* The teacher's role in Socratic Mentoring is to ask open-ended questions, to challenge ideas, to keep the dialogue focused, to involve as many students as possible in the discussion, and to summarise the main ideas covered.

Every opinion will be valued by the teacher, no matter how controversial or unconventional that opinion is. The great thing about this method is that it does not have to be limited to the study of philosophy. The Socratic Method can be applied to almost anything theoretical, whether it's learning about history, ethics, morals, politics, the environment or society. It is important that educators seek to apply this method often, in order to get students to strengthen their critical thinking skills and to challenge conventional ideas. The Socratic Method will be a major part of The Six Dimension Model for education.

SUSTAINABILITY

Sustainability education will receive a much greater focus in this model. It is so important for humanity to reconnect with nature and to stop turning a blind eye to the many crises facing the planet. The education system at present does not take our environmental reality seriously enough.

Environmental Impacts

Before the industrial revolution came along, our ecosystems were doing quite well. Sure, humans still killed each other in unnecessary wars, but at least we left the Amazon rainforest alone, didn't pollute our oceans and our atmosphere, and didn't have to deal with the threat of nuclear radiation. It might be unpleasant to consider the extent of the damage we are doing to the earth, but if we do not consider it, we will have a far more unpleasant reality – a world that cannot sustain us.

Children need to be informed of the situation we find ourselves in, with a focus on practical solutions at both the local and global level. They will learn about the intelligent management of resources, about the importance of biodiversity and the need to respect nature in all its forms. They will also learn to *reduce, reuse & recycle* with regard to waste management. More importantly, they will be empowered by the education system to bring about positive change if that is the path they wish to choose in life. The emphasis will be on open dialogue and The

Socratic Method will be utilised in this study wherever applicable.

Clean & Abundant Energy

Sustainability education will examine, in great depth, the many methods for producing renewable energy. Students will not only look at solar and wind power as sources of clean energy, but also geothermal, wave, tidal, sound, and zero-point energy technology. They will learn about alternative ways to power vehicles and other transport, such as electric cars and water-powered fuel cells. Children will be encouraged to invent new methods for renewable energy, and to come up with solutions for greater energy efficiency. As much as possible will be learned 'hands-on' through the investigative process and experimental inquiry.

Problem Solving

Students will learn to be problem solvers when it comes to the environment. Rather than simply learning the impacts human beings are having on the natural world, they will actively work on real practical solutions on both local and global levels – solutions that will be achieved through a collaborative process. Once these solutions are reached, schools will push to implement them in the real world. The children will see that their own ideas are of value and will come to realise their own power, while at the same time feeling like they have helped humanity in some way. We don't need more people to run the machines and do the paperwork. We need people who can see a problem that needs solving and say, 'I could come up with a solution to this problem and put that plan into action.' We need our kids to be able to analyse challenges and overcome them.

Immersion in Nature

Unless we are willing to encourage our children to reconnect with and appreciate the natural world, we can't expect them to help protect and care for it.

- David Suzuki

Children will learn about nature by getting amongst nature. We can't seek to intellectualise all of our learning. Learning must also be *felt*. When we try and learn about our environment indoors, there is a disconnect. Once children begin to immerse themselves in the natural world instead of being cooped up in classrooms, they will develop a closer bond with all living things. I think the reason why many of us turn a blind eye to our environmental problems is that we don't *feel* them. We don't feel the psychological torment of the baby orangutans whose parents are killed in industrial deforestation. We don't feel the pain of the seabird suffocated by oil. We don't feel the struggle of the Amazonian wildlife as they are faced with the destruction of their homes. If we're going to live sustainably on this planet and respect our ecosystems, we need to immerse ourselves in nature as the peaceful indigenous peoples of the world have done for many millennia.

Self-Sustainability

Sustainability is not just about maintaining a healthy planet and a healthy society, but also about sustaining ourselves as individuals. How do we become self-sustainable? By learning how to produce or create all our own basic needs to survive and thrive, without being dependent on any system to do that for us. This means that everything we take for granted - food, water, energy, shelter, comfort - we should be able to provide ourselves in a crisis. Right now, most of us buy our food from the supermarket or grocer, get our water from the water companies, get our energy from the energy companies, get our shelter from the State, and get our basic comforts from commercial industries. If the system went down due to a global economic collapse, a world war, or a natural disaster, few would know how to provide these basic needs themselves. I will admit, I would struggle myself. As a child of Generation Y, I never developed the skills to be able to fend for myself in times of great need. My parents never taught me and neither did the education system. If I have children one day, I will have a hard time passing on these skills to them. They will need to get them from elsewhere.

I'm aware that many people think this should be the parents' responsibility. To a large extent, I agree. However, the reality is that it is just not happening this way. Sadly, less and less parents appear to be taking the time to teach their children these life skills. How would we change parenting? As amusing as it may be, we can't have mandatory parenting classes or parenting licenses because that would be totalitarian. When it comes down to it, good parenting is a product of good societal values, and good societal values are a product of a good education system. Therefore, logic suggests that the best way to change parenting in the long term is to change the education system. For this reason, I see it as necessary for children to learn these skills from the education system, until parenting undergoes a transformation of its own. That being said, I wholly encourage all parents to teach their children as many meaningful life skills as possible, to prepare them for the obstacles life throws at them. It's important that we start to wean ourselves off the system – so that we know how to grow our own food, collect our own water, provide our own clean and abundant energy supply, build our own weather-proof homes using common materials, and anything else that allows us a fruitful, independent life, free from commercial exploitation.

Health & Wellbeing

Part of being self-sustainable is knowing how to look after your health. Schools will rarely enforce healthy lifestyle choices, but instead will make the necessary information readily available to all students, so that they can see how certain decisions are affecting their health. There will be more of an emphasis on the positive benefits of healthy habits, rather than the negative consequences of unhealthy ones. Children will learn how meditative practices and physical exercise are beneficial to their physiological and mental health. As part of this understanding of health and wellbeing, students will also undergo physical education classes to maintain their fitness while at school. Unhealthy foods will not be available within the school environment, so if children wish to eat them, they must come from home.

Children who take part in advanced cooking training will be given the opportunity to fine-tune their skills as school chefs, providing all kinds of delicious and creative lunches for the rest of the students. It is my hope that many roles of responsibility will be available to all students to give them a real taste for what it is like to contribute to a community. It is crucial for the children to feel like they are being treated as valuable members of the school by being trusted with important roles that directly impact on the functioning of the school.

Children will also receive a proper education about plant medicines and other natural remedies. They will learn of the healing powers of cannabis oil and how they can extract it themselves in a safe way. They will learn about particular foods, spices and other ingredients that can be used to treat physical ailments. They will learn about the various properties of psychoactive plants, as well as the positive and negative effects of consuming them. This includes an understanding of things such as ayahuasca, ibogaine, psilocybin and cannabis. These will not be practised in schools, but merely understood in great depth, so that children know of the various consequences of using them.

Teachers will be well-trained in understanding mental health issues and disabilities. Schools will provide places for children to go to talk through their mental health issues or to receive help and support in times of great need. Teachers will equip students with the skills to deal with situations where their peers are mentally or physically unwell. Schools will focus on showing empathy to those who are experiencing emotional hardships. Children will be encouraged to speak out and to make their concerns known rather than keeping any hurt to themselves. The school environment will be a place where all children feel accepted for who they are, no matter what they are going through in their lives.

INNOVATION

This dimension focuses primarily on human creativity, and how that relates to our progress as a species. Children will be encouraged to transcend the boundaries of convention at every turn and will be given every opportunity to hone their own creative impulses in any learning area they choose.

Divergent Thinking

The best ideas are often the most unconventional ones. The problem with the current education system is that convergent thinking strategies are fostered instead of divergent ones. Convergent thinking is regimented, linear and deductive. It only sees problems as having one answer, and you're either right or you're wrong. Tests, exams and other summative assessments generally fall under this type of thinking. Convergent thinking is restrictive and limiting to a child's cognitive development and drains them of their natural creativity. Don't get me wrong. There is a place for convergent thinking in schools, but it should not be the dominant problem-solving strategy. Divergent thinking looks at many possible solutions and requires us to delve deep into our imaginations. Human beings are naturally divergent thinkers from birth.

George Land and Beth Jarman, co-authors of the book *Breakpoint & Beyond: Mastering the Future Today*, conducted a longitudinal study of divergent thinking abilities in humans. They gave 1600 five year old children a test on divergent thinking and 98% of the sample scored at genius level. A divergent thinking test consists of problems that have multiple solutions, such as 'find as many different uses as you can for a paperclip.'

Land & Jarman tested the same children five years later (at age 10) and only 30% scored at genius level for divergent thinking. They tested the children again at age fifteen and only 12% excelled. A separate group of adults were given the same test and only 2% turned out to be divergent thinkers. Ken Robinson insists that the reason for this dramatic decline in creative ability over time is due to the fact we were *educated* in the traditional sense, and our natural creative impulses were hung out to dry instead of nurtured and developed. This is largely a result of the left-brain dominant model that rewards conventionality and discourages *out there* thinking.

In a new model for education, children will be encouraged to *think outside the box* in all aspects of their learning. They will be encouraged to challenge existing knowledge and to come up with imaginative and innovative solutions to any of the problems they face. 'Out of the box' thinking will be deeply ingrained in the educational philosophy of The Six Dimension Model, and all children's ideas will be respected and valued, no matter how controversial or *crazy* they may seem. The term 'crazy' is really just a way for the mainstream flock to label and criticise those who are different from the norm.

In a progressive education system that evolves out of the left-brain dominant paradigm, the 'ugly duckling' will not be alienated but celebrated. Creative play will allow children to sharpen these skills, as will the process of inquiry and the utilisation of the Socratic Method within the system's teaching format. We have to allow the young people of today to become the innovators of tomorrow.

Teaching Creatively

Part of teaching children how to be creative is to lead by example. Teachers should be looking for as many ways as possible to stimulate learning – ways which capture the children's imagination and sense of wonder. That sense of magic needs to be really alive in the school environment, as it ensures that learning is meaningful to the child. The more inventive ways a teacher can introduce a concept to a student, the more the student engages with the concept and connects intrinsically with what is being learned.

Furthermore, I argue that children who are exposed to a wide range of creative teaching methods are more likely to be creative problem-solvers as well. Children like to emulate the actions of their teachers, whom they often view as role models. It wouldn't make sense for a school to claim it nurtures creativity while teaching in mundane, habitual ways. Creativity must seep through into all aspects of school pedagogy. The most exciting and inspiring lessons are often the ones that seemingly come completely out of left field, and give children a unique experience unlike any other they have had before. It's so important to tap into a child's sense of wonder, especially in the younger years.

Collaboration

Schools will focus on collaborating in the learning environment instead of pitting students against each other or isolating them. Most work in class will be done in pairs or small groups. This nurtures a real sense of community in schools, and shows children the power of working together for a common goal. I came across this outstanding quote by Alfie Kohn, an author and educational commentator I have a great deal of respect for:

Any kind of competition is death to community because it trains students to look at their peers as rivals instead of allies.

Do we want to bring up our children to chase after success at the expense of other human beings? I think this is precisely what we have to *stop* doing. Competition is not an effective motivator in schools because it places the focus on the reward and not on the concepts being learned. Innovation is best realised through collaboration. We can achieve so much more when we work as a collective instead of as individuals. The pooling of minds is the stuff of greatness.

That's why it is my plan to give The Six Dimension Model to the brains-trust of all humanity as an open-source project online, so that we may work together to construct the very best education system our species could ask for. I can't come up with the solutions all on my own, and much of what is written in this book is subject to change. All I am doing is offering the skeleton; the chassis if you will. It will take the collective to make this system as meaty and robust as we can. If children learn to cooperate with one another and collaborate with one another all through their schooling, they will continue to do so as adults, and there will be no limit to what they can do. I really stand by that. Changing the paradigm from competitive to collaborative is one of the most important things we can do in terms of our own human evolution as well. I will revisit this concept later when I outline the structural aspects of a new education system.

Mathematics

Mathematics is only as necessary as its application in real life. Only a tiny sliver of students who get an education actually require math skills beyond about the age of ten. The rest can live a full and happy life without learning *any* of the high school mathematics curriculum. So much of mathematics in schools is decontextualized and seemingly pointless. There is no subject children are generally more resistant to than mathematics, and most of that resistance comes around the time students start learning algebra.

This new model proposes some drastic changes to the mathematics curriculum. Firstly, high school mathematics will be taught, but will be entirely optional. Only those who are primarily logical-rational learners or who have a passion for linear reasoning will be likely to elect to learn higher math, and that is exactly how it should be. Let the computing minds learn algebra while the creative minds write stories or play music. Those who do choose to do math at secondary level and enjoy it are likely to pursue work using those skills after they leave school. That is the way it should be, and we will always have people to do those math-intensive jobs. For the rest of the students, they will not forfeit a huge chunk of their adolescence to learn something that has absolutely zero bearing on their lives. I was a member of this camp, and I have never needed to use anything I learned in high school mathematics. Come to think of it, I don't even remember most of what I learned in high school mathematics... probably because it was so devoid of meaning to me.

Primary level mathematics only really needs to consist of basic numeracy, basic computations, basic decimals, basic fractions, shape, space, time and measurement. Even still, those should all be taught in ways that demonstrate their real-world application.

Another thing that needs consideration is for mathematics to stop being treated as a whole bunch of facts and rules that need to be memorised. The Socratic Method can be especially useful in teaching this subject, as it can deepen a child's understanding of math concepts, and get them to think critically about how certain terms are defined. After all, mathematics is just a construct we humans made up to help us make sense of what we see in the world around us.

Finally, geometry will receive a much greater focus in the primary math curriculum, so that children get a real sense for how mathematics relates to the fabric and structure of the universe itself. Once they see how the golden ratio, the Fibonacci sequence and basic equilateral shapes are all connected to each other and to the framework of reality, mathematics will be embraced, not just tolerated. Learning these geometrical concepts caters to both the left-brain (logical-rational) and the right-brain (abstract-emotional) learners, and makes the process of learning math so much more meaningful.

Science & Technology

Science should be taught through *inquiry* and *investigation*. For the most part, western education already recognises this. The best approach to teaching science is through hands-on learning. Children need to be able to make their own discoveries and figure out how and why things work or don't work, by experimenting in practical settings in small groups. Sadly, when I taught in a government school in Nepal, children learned science out of a textbook. I couldn't think of a less stimulating way to teach it. Some might argue that this is due to a lack of resources, but I would posit that a great many science experiments can be done with common objects found in the home or in nature. The problem was not the lack of resources, but the teaching pedagogy itself.

The best science teachers to me are the ones who ask probing questions and then let the children investigate those questions through a trial and error process, while encouraging the children to come up with their own questions and hypotheses to test as well.

The biggest problem I see with science education, and indeed with science in general, is that it tends to remain stubbornly inside the box. Science has a habit of defending its own knowledge. As soon as something is known or discovered, it is generally treated as gospel and never really questioned again. In this way, science has developed a certain arrogance that gets in the way of true scientific inquiry. As scientists and science teachers, we have to stop asserting we know all the answers and that anyone who suggests otherwise is simply wrong. That is not scientific wisdom. Socrates said, 'The only true wisdom is in knowing you know nothing.' Real science tries to prove itself wrong in every way. That is the direction that science education must go also. For example, if children are shown a real zero-point energy device that works in front of their own eyes, rather than finding every reason to say the inventor is a fraud or a charlatan because the machine disobeys traditional science, look at the reasons why that machine *is* working instead and have the children investigate those functions. My idea of a good science education is to get rid of the box completely. We don't need it. Science is like a canvas and we're constantly touching it up. The more we add to the canvas, the more the picture becomes clear, but it is a canvas we will never stop adding to, for the universe is likely infinite. Our young scientific minds ought to be driven by the idea of discovery and not by the ego.

COMMUNICATION

Understanding and connecting with one another, no matter our differences, is paramount to our evolution as a species. The better our ability to communicate, the easier it is for us to work as a collective and solve the world's problems together. Communication is about so much more than just written and spoken language, and children should have an understanding of language in all its forms.

Retaining our Native Languages

Diversity of language is a beautiful thing. It would be a sad state of affairs for us to lose our languages. English is the world's most influential language, but we wouldn't want it to completely replace our native tongues. At the same time, we need to make it easy to communicate with one another, no matter who we are or where we come from. Unfortunately, there is not always a translator present wherever we go. In places where English is standard, only English will be taught in schools as part of the mainstream curriculum. In places where English is not standard, English will be taught as a second language alongside the dominant native language. In places where there are lesser-known native languages, it will be up to the parents to teach their children in that tongue. If children desire to learn languages other than English or the region's native languages, other languages will be available to take on as voluntary studies in the same way that LOTE (Languages

Other Than English) studies are available in the current system.

Basic Literacy

So many children around the world are deprived of opportunities in life because they are illiterate. For most schools, basic literacy skills are a priority, as they open many doors that would otherwise remain closed. I think these skills are important as well, and a new education system should ensure all children are well-equipped to read and write. That said, literacy and language education should be voluntary beyond primary school level. Once a child can read fluently and get their message across effectively on paper (or the computer screen) it is no longer a necessity for all children to pursue an advancement of these abilities. Many students will not have a need for complex grammatical knowledge in their lives. Some will, and for them, they will have the option to go down that track as a voluntary study.

Basic spelling and grammar will be taught, but in ways that children can enjoy and appreciate, through things like interactive media. Learning spelling and grammar by rote will be abolished to make way for less archaic and more engaging contemporary methods.

In writing practice, attention will be given to developing the student's inner voice, rather than adhering to certain strict grammatical laws that do more to hinder expression than to heighten it. The best way to communicate is by being true to yourself. Provided the spelling is correct and the grammar is understandable to the reader, the inner voice should be unrestricted as much as possible. Readers would rather see unbridled passion in someone's writing than an academically precise watered-down version of their truth.

Media Literacy

In this day and age, where media is everywhere we look and pervades our lives at every turn, it is vital that we learn how to decode it in all its forms. Too many children are never taught how to read subtext, and they easily become victim to manipulation from advertising, news media and corporate interests. From around the age of ten, schools should expose students to all kinds of media, with the goal being to get children to think critically about the persuasive techniques at play. They should read articles in newspapers, watch commercial advertising, and listen to political speeches, to try and understand how the target audience is being manipulated by media. Ideally, poor journalism, corporate advertising, and corrupt leaders shouldn't exist, but because they do, we need to equip the next generations with the smarts to avoid their traps. If we can teach everyone to think critically about media, predatory corporations will no longer control us.

Emotional Recognition

From an early age, children should learn how to recognise a wide range of emotions in human beings. Through an understanding of body language indicators, children will become better at both responding to others' emotions and managing their own. They will learn how to effectively resolve conflicts and stop particular emotions from overwhelming them in their lives. Children should understand that all emotions are a normal, natural part of life, and that it is important to feel negative emotions at times as well. When students are skilled at recognising emotions, and become conscious of their feelings in everyday life, they will cultivate better relationships with everyone they interact with, and become better empathisers.

The Language of Life

Though the written and spoken word is essential for effective communication in the 21st century, there is a language far more fundamental to the universe and everything that exists within it. It is a language all things recognise. I call it *the language of life*. It is the lyrical song of the morning bird, the smiling eyes of a child, the sound of trickling water in a gentle stream, the swaying of trees in a cool summer breeze, the waxing and waning of the moon, the migration of penguins in the arctic, the percussiveness of a tribal dance... it is the very rhythm and expression of life itself. We cannot quantify it, we cannot intellectualise it, we cannot rationalise it, and we cannot teach it. This form of language can only be experienced. That is why immersing our children in the natural world as much as possible is paramount to their education. Our system need not focus on preparing the youth for what is to come later, but rather to show them what it means to live fully in the present moment.

Nature is a dance – it is a complex interweaving of syncopated rhythms, each with its own aesthetic signature. Once one is able to *feel* life in this way, it begins to mean so much more. Children have much to learn from the language of the world simply by connecting with it.

EMPATHY

The planet desperately needs more peacemakers, healers, restorers, storytellers and lovers of all kinds.
- Dalai Lama

Our species will only progress once we learn how to live together on this planet without killing, torturing and abusing one another. We have the ability to communicate across large distances wirelessly, yet we haven't worked out how to truly connect. We have the ability to feed, clothe and house every human being, yet we devote our energy to war instead. We have the ability to see galaxies millions of light years away, yet we can't even see eye-to-eye with each other. If humankind is to have any hope of evolving, children have to learn *empathy*.

Unity & Community

Embedded within the core values and philosophy of a new education system will be the understanding that we are all one planet. Nationalist fervour is poisonous to our growth. The idea that every nation is separate and alienated from all other nations does nothing but generate fear of the *other*. This new model will give no attention and no energy to nationalistic pride and will seek to abolish the current *us* and *them* mentality that has pervaded our way of life for millennia. Unity of our entire species will be embraced, but not uniformity. Uniformity abhors diversity whether as nature produces diversity. Diversity needs to be celebrated

as a natural, beautiful part of life. Every single human
being on this planet is unique. What makes us different
from each other should not be a reason to fear each other.
Children should learn the importance of loving each other
because of our differences, not despite them.

At the heart of the school system will be the
philosophy of Ubuntu – *I am because we are.* Selfishness will
begin to make way for selflessness. The system will not pit
students against each other in competition, but rather bring
them together to help one another. Schools will not be
institutions, but communities instead, where all members
are treated like family.

The 'Kin' school in Tekos, Russia, founded by Mikhail
Shchetinin, is one such school that embodies this all-
important sense of community. The children all designed,
built and decorated the entire school themselves. They
cook for each other, write the textbooks for the school
curriculum together, teach each other, collaborate every
day in groups, take on cleaning and maintenance duties
together, and elevate each other to reach their full
potential. At the end of each day, they get together as a
whole school to review their progress. As a result of this
community culture and inclusive philosophy, the students
are free-spirited and highly developed in all areas of
learning. There is much more to the Kin school than this,
and I recommend that anyone interested look into this
school in greater depth.

This is the kind of community that the education
system needs to be fostering all around the world. Allow
the children to contribute to every aspect of the school. Let

them ask the questions. Let them be the teachers. Let them create the environment they want to learn in. Make them feel valued, respected and trusted.

Consciousness

In order for children to understand how we are all connected on this planet, they need to learn about consciousness. As it stands, they are learning things only from a materialist, reductionist perspective, which limits human understanding to everything that can be experienced through the five senses. We now know that the universe is made up of an ocean of energy we can't touch, taste, smell, hear or see, so we have to expand our educational investigations to include a study of phenomena beyond materialist perception. The best way for children to learn about conscious awareness is through direct experience and scientific exploration.

Meditation practice gives the learner access to this field of consciousness, allowing them to experience an awareness outside of their own physical body – an awareness of all that exists in space and time. Meditation shows us that we are all of the same essence, and that what we do to another, we do to the self.

A new education system will look closely at the consciousness of plants, animals and even water, using the scientific method. Children should see how with a set of electrodes and a MIDI-synthesizer connected to an amplifier, a plant can be taught to express itself musically. At the Federation of Damanhur in Piedmont, Italy, these

experiments on plants have been carried out for over 30
years, which have proven that plants are sentient,
emotional beings capable of telepathic communication.
Students should also carry out Dr Masaru Emoto's
experiments on the effects of thoughts and intentions on
water, as well as devising their own hypotheses and testing
them. These are the kinds of hands-on projects that all
children would be fascinated by... the kinds of experiments
I wish I would have done as a child. Students should
examine the quantum world from all angles - from Tesla's
discovery of wireless electricity, to the nature of the unified
field, to a study of cymatics and vibratory energy. There is
much for them to discover about our vast and complex
universe through the process of inquiry and investigation.
It is these scientific revelations about consciousness that
give real weight to the understanding that *we are all one.*

Understanding the Individual

If education is to focus on empathy, teaching staff have to
lead by example. Teachers should be going out of their way
to establish a human connection with each individual child
under their wing. In the current system, many teachers
have a desire to do this, but find they are bogged down
with administrative tasks and regimented class formats
that restrict this one on one time. The structure of
traditionalist education does not allow for ongoing
personalised connection in the way that a progressive
education model could. As a result of this failing system, so
many children feel like their teachers don't care and have

no interest in getting to know who they are as a person. The Six Dimension Model proposes that all teachers really take the time to understand and connect with each student on a deeper level in order to better respond to their needs and interests, as well as establish mutual trust between staff and students. When a child decides to act out, the teacher needs to be responding by attempting to understand what it was that caused that child to act that way – to better understand how that child may have been feeling at the time, not by looking for the most effective way to reprimand that child. The teacher- student rapport needs to shift in this way in order for children to feel understood. By making this human connection, teachers show students that they value and respect them as unique and diverse beings.

Paying It Forward

When I was in my early teens, I watched a movie called *Pay It Forward.* In it, a young boy comes up with a revolutionary idea to change the world as part of a 7th Grade project in high school. His idea is to initiate three random acts of kindness and have each recipient pass on three more acts of kindness to others, triggering a chain reaction of love and compassion. The idea is brilliant in theory but would be difficult to really get going in societies due to the fact we have been programmed over many years to be selfish and competitive. However, if children were encouraged to pay it forward from an early age as part of the philosophy of their school, that is a different story. I can only begin to imagine how powerful such an educational philosophy would be in healing the wounds of humanity. Perhaps I am overstating it, but then again, perhaps I am not. One thing is certain... it can only bring about positive change, so there is every reason for schools to implement it.

The way a 'pay it forward' philosophy in education will work is twofold. First, schools encourage every student to go a little out of their way to do something good for another student once in a while, or as often as they wish. I stress the word *encourage* as this is not something that would be forced on the students by any means. Second, schools encourage each recipient of a good deed to pass on the favour to another student. There will be no official rewards or incentives for these deeds, other than the positive feelings associated with real human connection. After all, what could be a better incentive? It would also be a good idea for schools to ask students to reflect on and share how these acts of kindness made them feel.

I have no doubt that what you'll find is that students will carry this compassionate nature over into their adult lives. Rather than ignoring a homeless person, they will go out of their way to make sure that person has some food in their stomach. They will be more likely to help that old lady across the road, rescue an animal in distress, or reach out and hug a stranger who feels unloved. These random acts of kindness go a long way to healing the deepest of wounds, and the knowledge that someone truly cares about you can turn your life around. Everything starts with education. With the right educational philosophy, that shows kindness and compassion to all living beings, the world can be a place full of love and beauty.

Connecting to the Heart

Schools need to be equipping children with the skills to connect with one another emotionally, especially when children are in desperate need of that human connection. When a child hasn't personally experienced the same situation as one of their peers, it can be hard for that child to show empathy. In these scenarios, words are not likely to have very much impact. Sometimes, all a child needs to feel understood is a hug. Not just any hug, a *heart-to-heart hug* – one where both people raise their left arm instead of their right arm so that both hearts touch in the embrace. Hugging feels so much more powerful in this way and I think it is how we were meant to embrace one another naturally. Doesn't it make more sense to be hugging this way, seeing as human connection stems from the heart?

We don't hug enough as a society. Children should be hugging each other in school as a way of saying 'I'm here for you.' This whole 'keep your hands to yourself' doctrine has destroyed real, raw, positive human connection in schools. Political correctness has gone way too far and needs to be shown the door. There is nothing wrong with a teacher hugging a child or a child hugging a teacher. How sick is this society that we deny this kind of a connection in schools? There are many children who do not have a mother or father figure in their lives and look to their teacher for this connection.

I worked in a school in Melbourne where a Sudanese boy looked up to me as a father figure since he did not have a father of his own. Every day I came to the school, the boy would cling to me like glue and didn't want to leave my side. These kinds of children need a real heart-to-heart connection with their teachers as they aren't getting it anywhere else.

The power of a hug shouldn't be underestimated, but it's not the only way to respond to someone who is opening up to you and bearing part of their soul. Sometimes, it can mean the world to someone to sit beside them in silence and take on their pain as your own. When students learn about emotional recognition and body language, they should be role-playing various scenarios to gauge what kind of responses work best in different situations.

Our children need to start learning how to be loving, caring, compassionate and empathic human beings so that we stop looking for conflict everywhere we go and start working together for the betterment of the entire human family.

So, that's my outline for the six dimensions. The next section will be dealing with the *structure* of a new education system. Brace yourself, as I'm in favour of some pretty radical changes!

THE STRUCTURE

Non-Compulsory Attendance

Education does not need to be compulsory. Many families would prefer to educate their own children or have their children learn through experience in the world under their guidance. People may say that children won't turn up to school at all if it's voluntary. In a damaging educational environment such as today's dominant public school system I would agree, and I wouldn't blame them for their non-participation. If education was something children loved and if they got the chance to express who they were and felt a part of a community, there is no question that they would turn up to school every day.

The issue is not whether schools are compulsory, it's whether children have access to go to school or not. The reason there are so many illiterate children in many countries around the world is because they don't have access to school at all. All children should have access to good quality education.

Free Education for All

This is a given, but public education should be a basic right for all children, and that includes college and university education. I haven't really spoken of tertiary education in this book, as I'm more concerned with the elementary and high school systems, but putting university students into tens of thousands of dollars' worth of crippling debt is madness and has to end.

No Homework

You heard me. No homework. None. Zip. Zilch. Why would we put children through the ringer for an entire day and then make them forgo family time to do *more* work at home, on top of other household chores as well? Not in my book. School work should primarily be in the form of concept-driven collaborative group projects completed during school time.

No Standardised Testing

Of course, everyone reading this book knows that this is one of the first things that needs to be made unwelcome in a new education system. The whole world, bar our governments, would not lose any sleep over the abolishment of standardised testing protocols. It causes children to evaluate their own worth and their own intelligence by the same standards as everybody else. We can't compare children this way. As Noam Chomsky says, standardised testing is 'turning us into individuals that devote our lives to achieving a rank.' Standards will have no place in a new education system for humanity.

No Competition

Children should not be placed in an environment where their objective is to produce *better* results than the person sitting next to them. Competition in schools causes children to hold each other at arm's length, to distrust one another, to withhold information from one another, and above all, to take pride in superiority at the expense of another's inferiority. It drives the ego and distorts human connection. This is not a matter of reducing the amount of competition in classrooms, it is a matter of eliminating competition altogether. Children need to be working primarily *with* each other in pairs or small groups. Cooperation and collaboration will be at the heart of learning in a new education system.

Many people take the absence of competition to mean that one must be wandering aimlessly, without any goals. But competing simply means that one is working toward a goal in such a way as to prevent others from reaching their goals. This is one approach to getting something done, but (happily) not the only one. Competition need never enter the picture in order for skills to be mastered and displayed, goals set and met...

Cooperative learning is, in my judgment, one of the most promising alternatives to structural competition not just in the classroom but in any arena. If there is a single concrete image that represents the transcendence of mutually exclusive goal attainment, it is a picture of three or four children sitting around a table animatedly exchanging information and ideas.

- Alfie Kohn, *No Contest*

For anyone who thinks that competition is healthy, or an inevitable part of our human nature, I urge you to read Alfie Kohn's book, *No Contest*, as the research he has compiled proves otherwise. It is a book everyone should put aside the time to read, as it makes the case against competition crystal clear and will leave you in no doubt as to why education must adopt a cooperative approach to learning.

No Grading

Grading is just another form of competition. By giving children, say, a letter grade from A to F, you are ranking them from best to worst, or from smartest to dumbest. Grading systems take the focus away from the concepts and skills being learned, diminishing the intrinsic value of that learning, and placing all the focus on the reward of getting a high grade. Not only this, but the students who consistently receive poor grades develop major psychological problems and suffer from serious self-esteem issues throughout their lives. These children are made to feel worthless and are often discarded by the education system under the false pretense that they are not taking their education seriously enough. We need an education system that doesn't place children on a hierarchical continuum and is entirely supportive and nurturing of those children who learn in a multitude of different ways. We need an education system that doesn't reduce a child's value to a letter of the alphabet or a number between zero and one hundred.

Alfie Kohn makes a really strong point about grading as well:

The more students are motivated to get good grades, the more the depth of their thinking, the preference for challenge and the interest in learning tend to suffer.

No Rubrics

Rubrics are really just assessment standards that must be adhered to. As I am against any form of standardisation, due to the adverse effects it has on creativity and unconventional problem-solving, rubrics will be abolished from education.

A Constructivist Approach to Learning

It's time to move out of the archaic paradigm of behaviourism and into the progressive and highly effective paradigm of constructivism. Behaviourist teachers rely on a punishment and reward system with the goal being to achieve compliance. Every school I worked at in Melbourne, regardless of how affluent or progressive it was, used this approach all-too-often. It's bribery, plain and simple, and is no different from the kinds of psychological experiments Skinner conducted on animals to produce particular desired behaviours. Teaching in this way is taking 'the easy way out', and is not the mark of a quality teacher. I don't necessarily blame the teachers for going about their jobs this way because the reality is that

the whole school system is encouraging and reinforcing
this approach. Constructivism requires educators to be
more skilled at their jobs, and so they should be, as
children should always learn out of a desire for learning,
not because they get to go to lunch early or receive a gold
star for their efforts. The Socratic Method is built on a
constructivist approach and ensures that children are
constantly inquiring, investigating and autonomous over
their own learning. Provided children are intrinsically
motivated in this way, there is no need at all to fall back on
extrinsic rewards that cheapen the learning experience
altogether.

No Uniforms

So many schools all around the world have a school
uniform of some kind. Why? I can assure you it doesn't
add to a child's sense of belonging. School uniforms really
serve no practical purpose at all, other than being a way to
identify that students are from a particular school. Why
would they need to be identified when they spend all their
time enclosed within a perimeter fence all day anyway?
No, this is not a valid reason to have school uniforms. Most
children don't even like wearing them and relish casual
clothes days when they (rarely) come around. I detested
wearing a shirt and tie to school every day and having to
constantly pull up my socks over my knees. It was
demoralising for me to have to conform to someone else's
idea of how I should look for the vast majority of my
childhood and adolescence. It strips children of their

personal uniqueness and individualism, which are important for self-expression. I was fortunate enough to work in a Melbourne school that was the first of its kind here – a 'no uniform' school. Having no uniforms presented no problems at all. I could see how relaxed and at-home the children were in the clothes that they wanted to wear, and none of the children were distracted by their peers' clothing. Parents did not have to fork out their hard-earned money on school uniforms. The learning environment received a welcome splash of colour as a result as well. After having worked in this particular school, I cannot possibly see a reason to have school uniforms, and I strongly advocate against them in a new education system. Students of all ages should be allowed to express themselves freely through their appearance, and that includes hair styles, hair colour, piercings and tattoos. Universities don't have dress codes, so why do schools?

No Titles

Teachers do not need to have titles. All they do is give teachers this perceived power over students and inflate their own egos. Why should teachers be treated as any more important than children? We need to be on the same level and stop demanding that young people respect their elders. How about adults respect children for a change? Then we might get somewhere. Enough of this 'Sir, Mr, Mrs, Miss, Ms'… teachers should be addressed by their first names. It's more personal and children ought to have that kind of a connection.

Multi-Age Learning

Instead of regimenting the school structure based on age level (as if children have to be processed 'by their date of manufacture' as Ken Robinson puts it), schools will adopt a multi-age approach to learning. Fortunately, many schools are already moving towards this structure, but my hope is for it to be universally recognised and implemented. The multi-age learning environment consists of students spanning across different age levels and abilities, approximately two years apart. For instance, one class might be a mix of five year olds, six year olds and seven year olds, all learning at different paces and at different stages. Though you might be tempted to think that this kind of a learning environment would hold back certain learners from achieving excellence, the implementation of such a system in schools has shown that not to be the case at all. In fact, such an environment boosts performance levels all round. Within such a setting, teachers are able to group the children based on ability and preference for challenge. They are able to tailor specific learning tasks to the group or individual in order for every child to reach their maximum potential.

The older children act as mentors for the younger children and lift them up. Children get to experience socialisation in a way that is not available to them in the traditional K-12 grade structure, which is healthier for their overall development and sense of community within the school. At the elementary/primary level, they spend two extra years with the same classroom teacher in a multi-age setting, which is beneficial for their sense of connection, and allows the teacher to really get to know the needs of each student as the years go by.

This requires a higher standard of teaching, as teachers are having to constantly gauge and assess individual progress and diversify learning tasks, but we owe it to the future generations to hold our teachers to high standards. If we don't teach in this way, then we are continuing to teach to the *average* child, letting the low achievers slip and holding the advanced students back. Multi-age education should become the norm in every learning environment around the world.

Integration of Special Needs Students

The multi-age classroom is also the ideal learning environment for special needs children and children with learning disabilities, and ensures that these children are not being shunted off to one side or cast off into the 'special education' basket away from the other students. To prevent this kind of integration putting more pressure on the teacher, every classroom with special needs students will have Integration Aides – helpers who work with these children on a personal level, nurturing their development, assisting with ongoing assessment and mentoring them every day. It will be essential for the teacher to work collaboratively and communicate with the Integration Aides and vice versa, to be on top of the needs of those children and their educational progress. I worked in a school where there were Integration Aides at all grade levels and I could see how much support the special needs students were getting while at the same time feeling a strong sense of being included and accepted by all the students in the class.

A Humanist Philosophy

The educational system will never be more humane and effective as long as we're thinking about schools primarily in terms of preparing future employees. As long as economics, with all of the conditionality and competition involved in our economic system, is driving the way we teach kids, we are not really going to be doing what's best for the kids themselves.

- Alfie Kohn

Education has to cease being about economic pragmatism and start being about human need, human interest, and human progress. I believe we are in a time of great change – the likes of which our species has never seen in its long history. We simply cannot continue to sustain the capitalist model for very much longer if we hope to move forward in our evolution. We don't put our children through school so that the vast majority of them end up spending their entire lives working jobs that don't nourish their soul. We don't put our children through school so that they may act as the cogs in a machine that serves the needs of the few and not the many. We don't put our children through school so that they may look out for their own interests at the expense of others. We put our children through school so that they may learn about this thing we call 'life' and how they can become caretakers of this great earth we are living on. Or at least that *should* be why we put them through school. The Six Dimension Model will not indoctrinate children to take our places as the next lot of unquestioning worker bees. It will give them the opportunity to be the person they dream of being, the savvy and the smarts to deal with the challenges we face on this planet, the full capacity for independent thought and the compassion to help others in need.

To me, that is a real education...

The Time is Now...

This is the part where I talk about where we need to go from here and how we get there. What will I be doing to get The Six Dimension Model out there? What can *you* do to help shift the paradigm? Most importantly, what can *we* do as a species to transform this world and give the future back to our children?

I want to first talk about my own plan moving forward and the steps I will be taking to reach the goal of a new education system. I want to be absolutely transparent with everyone as I don't want there to be any confusion at all with regard to an action plan. When I first made the decision to dedicate my life to this pursuit, my immediate thought was to design a new model that puts the old industrial model to shame. I thought, it'd be much too hard to try and change the system from within through gradual policy reform, as the people who control the policies are inherently corrupt and only want change when it suits their profit-agenda. School policy reform has to go through

a number of different channels before implementation, and
it would be like wading through a never-ending sea of red
tape. Policy reform is the *least* likely way to rock the boat
when it comes to education. Though there are some things
we can realistically get into the current public education
system that will make a difference, and I wholeheartedly
urge everybody to do whatever they can in this respect, the
smarter game plan is to work *outside* the confines of the
system and to withdraw support for government-
controlled standardised education. We're absolutely
kidding ourselves if we think our governments are going to
do a damn thing about education. Last I checked, my own
country's education budget was slashed in favour of
defence spending and funding the air-strikes in Syria.
Politicians and governments do not have the answers for
us. The only way to make sure our children get a real
education is to *create* a real education system that is out of
reach of our failing political system. Now is the chance to
wipe the slate clean and start over. Buckminster Fuller once
said:

*You never change things by fighting the existing reality. To
change something, build a new model that makes the existing
model obsolete.*

I've designed the foundations of such a model but it's not
yet complete. In order to complete it I need humanity's
help. The next phase for me is to create an online hub
where I can open-source The Six Dimension Model as a
collaborative project. It will be set up in such a way that

anyone, no matter who they are, how old they are, or where they come from, will be able to contribute to the project and actively work on refining the details of the model itself. It will be a community where people can connect, share ideas and work on making this education model the best it could possibly be for the whole human family. This will be a chance for everyone to take an active role in creating the future of education for all of our children. I am not copyrighting this model. I am not trademarking it. I am not attempting to make a profit out of it in any way. It is not my intellectual property. Sure, it was an idea that came out of my head but now that idea belongs to the world. So don't wait for me to bring my plans to action. You have the model now. It's your model. Do whatever you can to get it out there. Start your own schools if you want. I don't care how you do it, just do it!

At the same time as starting this online hub, I will be looking for speaking platforms and writing platforms wherever I can. If you or someone you know run an independent radio show or host a public forum, I would be more than happy to be a part of it. Any way I can get the message out there and spread awareness about The Six Dimension Model will help move things in the right direction. I have provided my contact details towards the back of the book.

From there I will be looking to actually test the model over a number of years in a real school. It's all well and good having a robust theoretical blueprint but if you can't demonstrate to the world that it works in practice, you can't get the attention of the masses. I need to implement

the model in a real school setting and prove the benefits of
a new system to the world at large. Fortunately, an
opportunity has arrived for me to do just this, in no less
than a miracle. I will not disclose the details, suffice to say I
have contacts in a particular location to help me start up a
school system. The only reason I'm not saying more is
because I don't want to jeopardise the project and I don't
want to put anyone else involved at risk.
So what can *you* do to be a part of this mission and change
the current trajectory we are on?

The first thing you can do is withdraw your support
for the public school system. If you have the time and
energy, homeschool your kids! Give them the tools and
resources to become independent, critical thinkers. Help
them discover who they are at the core of their being. Find
out what it is in life that excites them and help them build a
life around that. Let them be as creative as they can be.
Nurture that need for self-expression. Show them how to
meditate. If your children are a little older, give them the
resources to discover how money is created and how
central banks control the money supply. After all, they
ought to not be kept in the dark about something that
controls almost every aspect of our lives. Most importantly,
teach your children to *question everything*. My three year old
niece's favourite phrase at the moment is 'But why?' Sure,
it can drive her parents mad when she uses that question to
try and delay bedtime, but that inquisitive nature is so
important in a child's development. She asks so many
questions and I fear for the moment in school when her
teachers tell her to stop asking questions all the time. No

child deserves to lose their sense of curiosity about the world.

I'm not saying you should be immediately ripping your child out of school and homeschooling them straight away. If they're already in school and have a vibrant social life with their peers, it would be harmful to take them out of that environment. Instead, you can teach them all those things I've mentioned above in your own little way outside of school time. Just subtly plant seeds for them to become free thinkers and show them that you support them no matter what path they desire to go down. If you're a parent whose child is in school, have a two-way conversation with your child and ask them what they would think about homeschooling. Explain the benefits to them and have a respectful dialogue about it. If they are resistant to the idea, don't push it further. If they're open to it, help them to transition to a homeschool environment. If you're a parent and you're yet to send your child to school, I urge you to really consider homeschooling. Same if your child is between schools or about to transition to high school. Again, work *with* your child, as a homeschool environment where the child is uncomfortable will be just as damaging as a government school. Make it fun for them. Give them freedom and flexibility. They will thank you for it one day.

If you don't like the idea of homeschooling, or don't have the time and energy, but don't want to send your child to a regular public school, consider an alternative school such as a Steiner school (Waldorf Education) or a Montessori school. I already mentioned the Steiner philosophy earlier in this book, so I won't say any more about that here, but I want to mention a little about the Montessori method. The Montessori method, invented by Italian physician and educator Maria Montessori, applies a hands-on approach to learning instead of direct instruction. Children learn primarily through inquiry and discovery within a multi-age environment. Maria Montessori designed a wide range of educational materials to help students explore and learn visually and spatially. The Montessori method offers a much more practical approach to academia than a child could get in a traditional government school. That said, the focus appears to be strongly on academic achievement, which is something that needs far less emphasis in education as I have already made clear. If you're interested in the hands-on approach to learning, I suggest you look into it further and consider sending your child to a Montessori school.

For all the teachers out there, you can make a massive difference in your own classrooms by moving away from direct instruction and instead pointing your children in the direction of the answers, without telling them the answers outright. I can't find the origin of this quote, but someone once said, 'The best teachers are those who show you where to look but don't tell you what to see.' Be one of those teachers.

Get meditation into schools any way you can! I can't stress this enough. Not only are the health benefits amazing, both physically and cognitively, but nothing else comes close to it as a tool for self-discovery. Teachers – introduce your classroom to simple breathing meditation. Sneak in 10-15 minutes at the beginning or end of a regular class if you can, several times a week. You will notice a marked difference in their overall focus and concentration, I assure you. Talk to your Principal about the prospect of introducing meditation into the whole-school environment. Make sure you do your research and outline the scientific studies behind the physiological benefits. Feel free to use the research I have compiled in this book as well. For people who live in the US, look into programs such as the MindUp program and The Inner Resilience Program, which are trying to bring mindfulness practices into American schools.

MindUp – www.thehawnfoundation.org/mindup
Inner Resilience – www.innerresilience-tidescenter.org

The advice I'm offering teachers goes for parents too. If you want to see meditation in schools, talk to your child's class teacher... talk to the school Principal... blow their minds with the research. If there are any meditation instructors or advanced meditation practitioners reading this book, talk to non-profit meditation organisations and see if you can arrange to go around to schools and offer a brief workshop for teachers and administrators. Campaign to get it into schools in any way you can. Spread the word in any way you can. Start a movement if you like! I will be spreading the word about bringing meditation into schools at every opportunity I can as well.

To all the garage inventors – get new energy technology out into the world. If you can replicate an energy device that has already been made before, or design a new one, then open-source the plans and distribute them to everyone. Don't give the energy companies a chance to suppress the technology. Don't try to patent it and profit off it. Give it to humanity for free. We have the means to control our own energy supply, move everybody off the corporate energy grid for good, and alleviate world poverty, so what's the delay? Let's get the tech out there!

Get informed about the central banking pyramid scheme and then inform others. Some quality resources that outline the fraudulent debt-based banking system in greater detail are:

> - *Zeitgeist* (Documentary)
> - *Zeitgeist: Addendum* (Documentary)
> - www.corbettreport.com/federalreserve
> - Thrive (Documentary)

Call for an honest debt-free monetary system. Demand that we take the power of money creation away from the central banks and give it back to the people. Another initiative you can get behind and support is a 1% tax levy system so that 1% of every transaction goes back to the treasury. This would apply to everyone including large corporations, and would put more money in everybody's pocket, free us all from debt, and mean we'd have to work fewer hours to earn our keep. Of course, this wouldn't solve many of the world's problems that are caused by profit-based capitalism, but it would be a big step in the right direction. The main objective should be for us to work towards a world without money altogether.

If, like me, you want to see a world of complete abundance where everyone contributes their acquired skills and talents for the benefit of their community, get behind Michael Tellinger and the Ubuntu movement. The movement is growing fast with a very strong support network and Tellinger is always looking for more people to represent the movement within their own country. Get involved in the burgeoning contributionist communities around the world. Once enough communities adopt this model, the rest of the world will have no choice but to start following suit in order to compete with the dirt-cheap produce in these communities. I have enormous faith in contributionism being the future of humanity. One day our species will look back through history and say, 'I can't believe humanity was controlled by pieces of paper and numbers on a screen.' The things we need to survive are not scarce but money creates artificial scarcity. Why would we continue to submit ourselves to such a damaging system?

We can do so much more!
To support the Ubuntu movement, go to:

www.ubuntuplanet.org

Spread awareness of The Six Dimension Model if it resonates with you. Tell your spouse, tell your kids, tell your friends and neighbours, tell the postman... make sure everyone knows that there is a much better way to educate our kids that will put an end to the indoctrination happening in schools today. Like I said earlier in the book, the model isn't perfect, but it's a hell of a lot better than what we've got, and with an open-source project, we can turn it into something truly remarkable for the whole human race. I'm calling on you to back me so we can all make this model a reality.

If you want to see change, then it must first come from within. Step into your power. Realise your true potential for this world. When I was a kid, I never saw myself as a leader. I saw my peers take on leadership positions at school while I stood on the sidelines and watched. I was a follower. I let others make decisions for me. I felt powerless to do anything but toe the line. Then one day I awoke from that prison I'd put myself in and my entire life changed. I realised that I had the potential to do so much more with this gift of life I'd been given. I'd been selling myself short. I knew that I had the power to make a massive difference in the world. At that moment, when I understood my true potential as a human being, I made a decision that I wasn't going to allow myself to be anything less than who I was capable of being. The point I'm making here is that we *all* have this potential. We *all* have this power. The future is not something that we wait for. We *create* the future. We are the writers of this story. We choose what happens to us in the next chapter. If we want our children to grow up in a world where they are not oppressed and enslaved, it is up to *us* to create that world.

Find that power that resides deep inside you. Stop living the life others want you to live and start living the life *you* want to live. Be the person you dream of being.

Take a risk. Quit your job if you have to. Abandon your studies if they aren't serving you. Don't let anyone else try and fit you into a neat little box. Take a leap of faith and don't look back. Summon the warrior spirit within! You are not just a flesh vehicle with a name and a passport. You are infinite conscious potential...

If you dream of a better world, then stand up and speak your truth. Boldly go against the grain. Say what others are too afraid to say. Fear is the only thing holding us back from real change. Step out of fear and step into love. When you see a homeless person on the street, don't just walk past them. Ask them if they're hungry. Get them something to eat. If they're cold, get them a blanket or some warm clothing. If they're out in harsh weather, help them find shelter. Ask them their name. Have a conversation with them. Listen to their story. Give them a hug they will never forget and tell them you love them! Look into their eyes and see just how much of a positive effect you had on their life. You will never forget that look, I promise you. Once you experience how it really feels to give something to another human being, you will rarely miss a chance to give. I'm not talking about the kinds of gifts you give at Christmas time or the money you donate to charity. I'm talking about *real* one on one human connection. We can turn this world around by simply looking after all our brothers and sisters on this planet. In the same way that it takes only one ripple to affect an entire ocean, it only takes one random act of kindness to affect the entire stream of consciousness. Don't wait for someone else to make the world better. Change starts with you...

The time has come to take matters into our own hands. We can't continue to give all our power away to the politicians, bankers and corporations. We have to stand up for our rights as living, breathing, loving human beings. We have to stand up for our children and our grandchildren. We have to stand up for the future of our species on planet Earth. Now, more than ever, we need a change in education. We need to put an end to the indoctrination in schools. We need to put an end to the suppression of our most natural, creative urges and impulses. We need a new education system that seeks to unite and empower our children. We need to take back our future.

The education revolution is now.

Join me

CONTACT

If you would like to get in touch with me, please send all correspondence to the following email address:

thesixdimensionmodel@gmail.com

You can also follow my Facebook author page and find me on Twitter:

www.facebook.com/thesixdimensionmodel

www.twitter.com/6dimensionmodel

—

REFERENCES

ALMOG, B. *Dr. Boaz Almog: Quantum Levitation.*
https://www.youtube.com/watch?v=4HHJv8lPERQ, The UP Experience, 2012.

BANKI, L. *Memoirs of a Madman 38.*
https://www.youtube.com/watch?v=h0dhwlhTs9M, Free Energy Documentary,
2007.

BERNAYS, E. *Propaganda.* pp. 9-10, 1928.

BOSTON DYNAMICS ROBOTS. http://www.bostondynamics.com/

BROWN, A. *This Minnesota Mom is Facing 2 Years in Jail for Saving her Son's Life.*
http://thefreethoughtproject.com/minnesota-mom-facing-2-years-jail-saving-sons-
life/, November, 2014.

BUSINESS INSIDER AUSTRALIA. *These 6 Corporations Control 90% of the Media in
America.* http://www.businessinsider.com.au/these-6-corporations-control-90-of-
the-media-in-america-2012-6, 2012.

CHENEY, M. *Tesla: Man Out of Time.* Barnes & Noble Books, pp. 157-158, 2001.

CHONG, T. *Tommy Chong Talks Treating Cancer with Cannabis.*
https://www.youtube.com/watch?v=ckY7Of3NMeg, August 2014.

COULTER, D. *Developing Nuclear Fusion in a Basement with a Reclusive Gunsmith.*
https://www.youtube.com/watch?v=ilOZ_aMrKos, Motherboard, VICE, 2014.

DASH ROBOT. http://dashrobotics.com/

DINGEL, D. Local Filipino TV Program on Water-Powered Car,
https://www.youtube.com/watch?v=UVhXrvCCILw#t=170

EVACUATED TUBE TRANSPORT. http://www.et3.com/

FRESCO, J. *Paradise or Oblivion.*
https://www.youtube.com/watch?v=KphWsnhZ4Ag, 2012.

FRESCO, J. *The Venus Project* (Website). https://www.thevenusproject.com

FUKUSHIMA CRISIS. *Negotiation with TEPCO / Japanese Government.* https://www.youtube.com/watch?v=Hwn1PU6GiPQ, June 6, 2013.

FULLER, B. *Synergetics: Explorations in the Geometry of Thinking.* Macmillan Publishing Co. Inc., Section 503.03 -503.031, 1975.

GARDNER, H. *Frames of Mind – The Theory of Multiple Intelligences.* Basic Books, 1983.

GREER, S. Interview from the *Thrive* (2012) Documentary. http://www.thrivemovement.com/the_movie

GOLDWATER, B. *With No Apologies.* Berkley, p. 281, 1980.

GOYAL, M., SINGH, S., et al. *Meditation Programs for Psychological Stress and Well-Being.* JAMA Internal Medicine, 2014.

HAGELIN, J. *On Consciousness and Super String Unified Field Theory.* http://www.hagelin.org

HITCHENS, C. *Letters to a Young Contrarian.* Basic Books, p. 3, 2005.

IDOGAWA, K. *Fukushima disaster: Tokyo hides truth as children die, become ill from radiation – ex-mayor.* http://rt.com/shows/sophieco/fukushima-disaster-radiation-children-740/, Sophie & Co, Russia Today (RT) Report, April 21, 2014.

INTERNATIONAL ENERGY AGENCY. *Report on global solar energy target for 2050.* http://www.iea.org/newsroomandevents/pressreleases/2014/september/how-solar-energy-could-be-the-largest-source-of-electricity-by-mid-century.html, September 29, 2014.

JOE CELL. http://www.byronwine.com/files/The Joe cell.pdf, article by Barry Hilton, 1998.

JOE CELL. *The Story of the Joe Cell.* https://www.youtube.com/watch?v=mAbuHe9X_cs, Documentary written by Charles Mansfield, produced by Airtime Productions & North Horse Media,

JOSEPH, P. *Zeitgeist.* https://www.youtube.com/watch?v=k3Ya5qiiW6k, 2007.

KIVA SYSTEMS ROBOT. http://www.kivasystems.com/

LAZAR, S., KERR, C., et al. *Meditation Experience is Associated with Increased Cortical Thickness*. Osher Institute, Harvard Medical School, Boston, MA, 2005.

MALLOVE, E. *Cold Fusion: Fire from Water* (Documentary, 1998)

MALLOVE, E. *Cold Fusion and Beyond*.
https://www.youtube.com/watch?v=6y98YwJ2GEE, Interview for Steven Greer's Disclosure Project.

MEYER, S. *Stanley Meyer's Sister and Niece Talk about his Death*.
https://www.youtube.com/watch?v=Bc7TCyhYd6M, Telephone Interview, 2013.

MODERN MONEY MECHANICS.
https://archive.org/details/ModernMoneyMechanics, Federal Reserve Bank of Chicago, p. 6.

MORAY, T. *The Sea of Energy in Which the Earth Floats*. http://free-energy-info.co.uk/P26.pdf, p. 55, 1960.

PAGNONI, G., & CEKIC, M. *Age Effects on Gray Matter Volume and Attentional Performance in Zen Meditation*. Department of Psychiatry and Behavioral Sciences, Emory University, Atlanta, GA, 2007.

PAUL, R. *End the Fed*. Grand Central Publishing, p. 202, 2009.

PUDDICOMBE, A. *All it Takes is 10 Mindful Minutes*.
https://www.youtube.com/watch?v=qzR62JJCMBQ, TED Talks, 2013.

REPRAP PROJECT. http://reprap.org/

ROBINSON, K. *Changing Education Paradigms*.
https://www.youtube.com/watch?v=zDZFcDGpL4U, RSA Animate & TED Talks, 2010.

ROBINSON, K. *The Element: How Finding Your Passion Changes Everything*. Penguin Books, p. 16, 2010.

RUNDLE, G. *A Revolution in the Making*. Affirm Press, p. 195, 2014.

SANTAYANA, G. *Life of Reason: Reason in Common Sense*. Scribner's, p. 284, 1905.

SAVIONE ROBOT. http://www.savioke.com/

SCHIFF, R. *Burzynski: Cancer is Serious Business.*
https://www.youtube.com/watch?v=rBUGVkmmwbk, 2011.

SCHNEIDER, R., GRIM, C., RAINFORTH, M., et al. *Stress Reduction in the Secondary Prevention of Cardiovascular Disease.* Institute for Natural Medicine and Prevention, Maharishi University of Management, Fairfield, IA, 2012.

SHELDRAKE, R. *The Sense of Being Stared At: And Other Aspects of the Extended Mind.* Arrow Books, 2004.

SILVA, F. *Secrets in the Fields.* Invisible Temple Publishing, Ch. 8, 2002.

SIMPSON, R. *Run From the Cure* (2008).
https://www.youtube.com/watch?v=0psJhQHk_GI

STRASSMAN, R. *DMT: The Spirit Molecule.* Park Street Press, 2001.

SUTTON, A. *The Federal Reserve Conspiracy.* CPA Book Publisher, p. 84, 1995.

TAYLOR, J. *Think Again: A Philosophical Approach to Teaching.* Continuum International Publishing Group, p. 23, 27, 2012.

TELLINGER, M. *Ancient Technology and the Ubuntu Movement.*
https://www.youtube.com/watch?v=gcD1h9DYitg#t=12, Breakthrough Energy Movement Conference, Holland, 2012.

TELLINGER, M. *Ubuntu Contributionism: A Blueprint for Human Prosperity.* Zulu Planet Publishers, South Africa, 2013.

TELLINGER, M. *Ubuntu Planet* (Website). http://www.ubuntuplanet.org/

TESLA, N. *Experiments With Alternate Currents of Very High Frequency and Their Application to Methods of Artificial Illumination.* Lecture before American Institute of Electrical Engineers, Columbia College, New York, May 20, 1891. (Original transcript from *The Inventions, Researches and Writings of Nikola Tesla*, by Thomas Commerford Martin, pp. 145-197)

THOREN, T., & WARNER, R. *The Truth in Money Book.* p. 24, 1980.

TOLLE, E. *The Power of Now.* Namaste Publishing, p. 123, 1999.

TOMPKINS, P., & BIRD, C. *The Secret Life of Plants.* HarperCollins, pp. 5-14, 1973.

VANDERLIP, F. *From Farm Boy to Financier.* D. Appleton-Century Co., pp. 210, 213-217, 1935.

VESPERMAN, G. *Energy Invention Suppression Cases.* http://www.byronwine.com/files/Gary%20V.pdf, 2007.

WATTS, A. *Live Fully Now.* https://www.youtube.com/watch?v=HdqVF7-8wng, Tragedy and Hope, 2014. (original audio recording from Watts' *Essential Lectures* series, 1960)

WILLIAMS, B. *Joe Cell Truck Builder Threatened, Destroys Plans.* http://pesn.com/2006/04/13/9600257_Bill_Williams_threatened/, 2006.

WILSON, W. *The New Freedom: A Call for the Emancipation of the Generous Energies of a People.* Gray Rabbit Publishing, Ch. 8, 2010. (original quote from 1913)